COAL MINES ~~~~~~~
ACCRINGTON
AND BLACKBURN

by

Jack Nadin

A
MONOGRAPH
OF THE
NORTHERN MINE RESEARCH SOCIETY
DECEMBER 1999

ISSN 0308 2199

ISBN 0 901450 51 0

© J. Nadin 1999

Typeset in 10 point Times New Roman

by

N.M.R.S. Publications

PRINTED

by

FRETWELL
PRINT AND DESIGN

Healey Works,
Goulbourne Street, Keighley,
Yorkshire, BD21 1PZ

for the publishers

THE NORTHERN MINE RESEARCH SOCIETY
KEIGHLEY, U.K.

Cover Illustration:
Eccleshill Colliery and Pipeworks (By permisson of Ann Stokes).

CONTENTS

FIGURES

PLATES

Editor's note

Many of the newspaper reports used in this publication were written in the long-winded style beloved of the Victorians. Where possible, I have cut out repetitions and rewritten parts of the reports in a more accessible style. No facts or names have been cut out, however, and, should anyone wish to read the originals, the name and date of the newspaper are given in every case.

ACKNOWLEDGEMENTS

I am grateful for the willing help given by the staff at Accrington and Darwen reference libraries. I am also grateful to: Harry Tootle of Oswaldtwistle for information and loan of photographs; Gordon Hartley of Burnley for loan of a number of newspaper cuttings relating to mining in the Blackburn area, uncovered during his research, and for the loan of a number of photographs; Alan Davies and staff at the *Lancashire Mining Museum* for their time and for permitting me to use their library; Ann Stokes of Darwen for a great deal of information on the Hoddlesden Collieries and, in particular, their founders, Joseph Place and Sons; Trevor Longworth, Middle Scotland Farm, Hoddlesden, for a potted tour of industrial Hoddlesden and district during which he pointed out various coal mining remains, and for the loan of photos; and Hazel Martell and Mike Gill of the Northern Mine Research Society for sorting the wheat from the chaff and publishing this book. Last, but not least, I must thank my wife Rita for her patience during my many hours of absence doing field studies in search of old mines and for the supply of refreshment while I have been endlessly stuck in front of the computer.

INTRODUCTION

The author's first book, British Mining No.58, *The Coal-Mines of East Lancashire*, dealt with coal mining in that part of the North-East Lancashire Coalfield between Colne and Padiham. This companion volume covers the townships of Church, Accrington, Oswaldtwistle, Baxenden, Blackburn and Lower and Over Darwen, which are to the west.

Readers should note that, particularly in the Darwen area, there were scores of shallow pits, shafts and drifts working during the early to mid 1800s. They appear on the 1844 OS Map, but identification of an individual pit is almost impossible. In many cases the sites were incorporated into the town as it developed, or became sunken hollows on bleak moorland. The more important sites have been recorded, along with a number of minor ones, and I apologise for any omissions.

The history of coal mining in this area goes back to at least the 15th century as, in 1409, the mines of coal and stone in the forests of Blackburnshire were recorded as being worth 14s 4d per annum. Three centuries later, during the reign of Queen Anne (1702-1714), a number of the inhabitants of Darwen were described as coalers and coal-getters. In 1729, Peter Walkden, a Nonconformist minister from Chipping, recorded in his diary for December 17th: *Son John went to Eccleshill coal-pit for two loads of coal.* This was a distance of some 30 miles and carriage was by sacks hung over the sides of horses and pack-mules. The *Manchester Mercury*, on July 22nd 1766, recorded that the manor of Over Darwen was to be sold on August 28th, adding that: *Under most of the estate there is coal, and the purchaser will be entitled to the Common Right of about 300 acres, under which there is also coal.*

Large-scale coal extraction, however, began at the turn of the 19th century, when deeper pits and surface haulage systems were developed to supply the rapidly developing mills and foundries, and by 1851 some 444 men and boys worked in pits around Darwen alone.

Unlike the South Lancashire and Wigan Coalfield, the area covered by this book suffered no great disaster, but death and serious injury were never far away. Local newspapers carry many short reports of deaths at the area's collieries and I make no excuse for including them, shocking though they may be, for they are often the only reference to a particular pit. They give many details of how the colliery worked, the depth of its shaft(s), the height of the roads and seams, and often the owner's name. Perhaps more importantly, they record some of the terrible conditions the miner endured underground, but the sadness and the grief behind such reports at the loss of a father, son or husband can only be imagined. In almost every such case no compensation was awarded, and it was accepted as a fact of life that one might expect to be killed or crippled when working down the pit.

The reader may be surprised to find that, in the early 19th century, not only mature men but also many young boys and girls of junior school age were killed in the pits, and this report from the *Blackburn Standard* for June 14th 1843 is not unique.

An inquest was held at the Millstone public house in Over Darwen into the deaths of Peter Radcliffe and John Harwood aged 13 and 9 years. They were employed as drawers in a coalmine owned by Jabez Kay, and on Friday morning they went to a place to mine coal, being farther than they ought to have gone, and where they were forbidden to go. The place was considered unsafe, and when they were getting coal from a pillar a portion of roof about 6 yards square and about 18 inches thick fell upon them. The alarm was given by some other boys, who had tried to prevent them from going into the place. They were got out in about 15 minutes, but both were dead. The inquest recorded a verdict of Accidental Death.

This inquest was followed by a court case because an Act of Parliament, passed the previous year, forbade the employment underground of all females and any boys under 10 years of age. The case was dismissed on a technicality, however, because it was uncertain who owned the pit. The price of coal was indeed high, in terms of human life.

Lancashire's coal mines, along with the horrors of children working underground in Britain, have long gone, but it has been said that history overlaps the present. Now we import much of our coal, some of it from countries where, we conveniently forget, children are employed in the mines. I dedicate this book to the fading memory of the coal miners of East Lancashire, and in particular to the young victims killed and maimed there.

THE MINING COMPANIES

GEORGE HARGREAVES & COMPANY

This company, which ran many of the Accrington, Baxenden and Rossendale collieries, was founded to work the copyhold mines in the manor of Accrington along with the Forest of Rossendale. Greater detail can be found in R.S. Crossley's *Accrington Captains of Industry,* published in 1933.

One of the first leases, dated April 1805, is an agreement between the Duke of Buccleugh, as Lord of the Manor, and Henry Hargreaves of Newchurch in Rossendale. Henry died in 1829, and his son, George, succeeded him. At this time there was practically no coal coming into the Accrington district. A further lease, taken in 1825, had a clause binding the lessees to *"use their best endeavours to get and raise coal and cannel sufficient to supply the consumption of the county."* In accordance with this, George Hargreaves and his partners, Richard Ashworth and Johnathan Hall, sank new drift mines and shafts along the hillside. Ashworth died around 1860 and Hall some years later, so the partnership was dissolved in 1867 and from then on was known as George Hargreaves and Co.

George Hargreaves asked John Hargreaves, who ran the Broad Oak printworks, to enter into partnership with him and seek a new lease from the Lord of the Manor. The printworks was an extensive employer and, perhaps more importantly, a large user of coal. A new lease was obtained, and Henry Hargeaves Bolton, a nephew of George Hargreaves, was appointed to the management. From this time forward the firm was closely connected with the Bolton Family.

In 1874, H.H. Bolton, Peter Wright Pickup, Thomas Brooks, a colliery and quarry owner of Rawtenstall, and the Burnley firm of the Exors of John Hargreaves formed the Dunkenhalgh Colliery Company Ltd. In November 1929, George Hargreaves (Collieries) Ltd. amalgamated with the Altham Colliery Company and Hargreaves Collieries (Burnley) in running the collieries and Altham Coke Works at Clayton-le-Moors. The firm then dominated the East Lancashire Coalfield until nationalisation on January 1st 1947.[1]

The following article gives some interesting historical information on local mining families:-

Accrington Observer, January 4th 1947:- *For several generations, in some cases going back nearly 150 years, the collieries in this area have been in the hands of a few families, who have retained their interest right down to the end of 1946. Although the firms have been converted into limited companies, the actual ownership has not changed because all the shares were retained by the families previously owning the pits, the descendants or legal representatives of the original owner. In Burnley, the Thursbys, direct descendants of Colonel John Hargreaves, and the Brooks of Towneley*

Plate I.
G.W. Macalpine (J. Nadin)

Collieries; in Accrington and Rossendale, the Hargreaves and Boltons,related to the original George Hargreaves; and in Altham, the Barlows and Macalpines, have continued in real ownership. This has brought about a degree of familiarity and generally friendship between owners and workmen and it is one of the regrettable features of Nationalisation that this personal relationship is brought to an end. There has never been any difficulty of access to the owners by the miners and, especially amongst the older workmen, there is some feeling of sorrow at the parting. Of the previous owners the only one to become an official of the Coal Board is Colonel G.G.H. Bolton, MC, DL, who is now Marketing Director for the North and West Division (Lancashire, Cheshire and North Wales). All the fuel sold in this wide area will now pass through his hands. Geoffrey Macalpine, JP, formerly managing director of the Lancashire Foundry Coke Co. Ltd, is not taking a post under the Board, as to do so would involve resignation from all the other directorates he holds. Perhaps the one to whom the change will be greatest is Mr George C.M. Barlow, chairman of Hargreaves Collieries Ltd, and of the Lancashire Foundry Coke Co. Ltd. He started work for the old Altham Colliery Co. over 65 years ago and, when the North East Lancashire Collieries were merged in 1932 to form

11

PLATE II Col. G.H. Bolton (Harry Tootle).

Hargreaves Collieries Ltd, he became chairman. But, although he might have had a post under the Coal Board, he feels that at his age it is undesirable to take on new duties as he is also a director of several other companies in Lancashire. Since its inception in 1935, he has been vice-chairman of Lancashire Associated Collieries, which until now has controlled the sale of the coals produced in the county. He has also been the president of the Lancashire and Cheshire Coal Association, and has held many other posts in the trade associations connected with the coal, coke, brick and tile industries. He was the first president of the National Building and Engineering Brick Federation, the third of the National Clay Federation, and the founder of the Northern Brick Federation.

SIMPSON & YOUNG

Another important colliery company was formed by Thomas Simpson, son of William Simpson, whose brother James had strong connections with the Foxhill Bank printworks at Oswaldtwistle. In 1837 Thomas Simpson and two cousins, Lawrence Rawstron and James Simpson Young, acquired the printworks at Foxhill Bank. Around this time, Simpson and Rawstron also began mining coal for the nearby mills. Within a few years the colliery company had the majority of pits in and around Oswaldtwistle. By 1850, presumably after the death of Lawrence Rawstron, James Simpson Young was an associate, and the partnership then became Simpson and Young. Thomas Simpson married Ellen, daughter of Benjamin Walmsley, a cotton manufacturer of Paddock House. Their son, William Walmsley Simpson, also went into colliery management. Thomas took a keen interest in the development of the collieries and, through skilful management, developed the Broadfield, Aspen and Lower Darwen collieries. Thomas lived on the simplest of food, and one of his greatest interests was the allotments in the Mill Hill districts, still known as Simpson's Gardens. He lived in

12

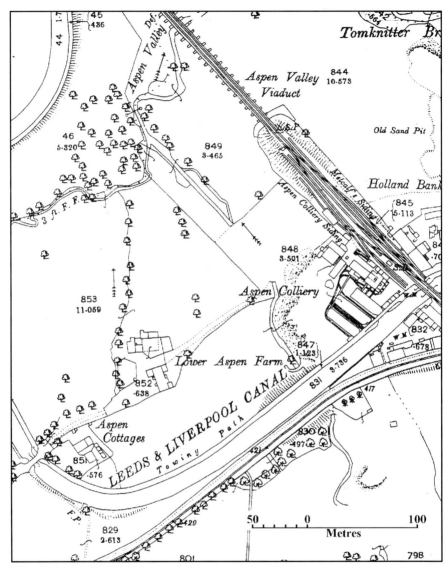

Fig. 1 Aspen Colliery.

Oswaldtwistle for many years, but he died at Oak Hill, Accrington, on January 31st 1875 aged 87 years. The Tables compiled by John Gerrard, Inspector of Mines for the Manchester District, in his 1896 Report still listed T. Simpson as owner of Aspen Colliery. In 1899, however, the business was taken over by Oswaldtwistle Collieries Ltd, whose principal partners were John Tomlinson, a Darwen colliery agent, Dennis Hayworth and William Sandeman.

COAL MINES AROUND ACCRINGTON AND BLACKBURN

ASPEN COLLIERY   SD737255

The colliery site, to the left of the Leeds and Liverpool Canal at Oswaldtwistle when walking towards Church, is best reached from the lane by the Hare and Hounds public house. Ruined coke ovens, along with a partially restored canal basin, can still be seen. According to the *Accrington Observer*, February 4th 1978, the coke ovens were proposed for listing as ancient monuments. Large engine beds, with recesses for the fly wheels, and the embankment of the colliery railway sidings can also be seen.

Aspen was one of Thomas Simpson and Co's larger mines. Between 1868 and 1869, they sank two 330 foot deep shafts to the Lower Mountain Mine, which here had an average thickness of 1 foot 9 inches. Listed in *The Collieries of Lancashire in 1879*, the company office was at 1 Rhyddings Street, Oswaldtwistle.[2] Thomas Scholes was the manager, with 79 men underground and 33 men on the surface in 1896. The colliery was closed in 1922, and its remaining coal was raised at Town Bent Colliery, until that too closed through exhaustion in 1925. Much of the coal was transported on the Leeds and Liverpool Canal, but the map of 1894 shows that the colliery had railway sidings to the SE of Aspen Valley Viaduct. The first fatalities were recorded when the shafts were being sunk.

Accrington Times, Saturday May 8th 1869:- *On Thursday a man was killed and 2 were seriously injured in an explosion at the new pit which has been sunk at Aspen, near Church. Three shifts of workmen are employed at the pit. One of them, consisting of 4 men, began work at 22.00 on Tuesday, and, when they had drilled a hole preparatory to blasting the rock, they fired a fuse and came to the top of the pit, which is about 60 yards deep. They remained on the pit brow about 15 minutes and, when no explosion had taken place, they concluded that the fuse had missed firing the powder, and went down again. They began to empty the drill hole in order to put in another fuse, but the explosion then took place, and Peter Hartley, 26, single, of Green Howarth, was instantly killed. Joseph Townley, 39, married and of Stanhill, was so seriously injured about the face and throat that his life is despaired of.* [He later died of his injuries.] *A man named Pickup, of Rishton, was also injured, and it is feared he will lose his sight. Richard Thompson, another workman, escaped unhurt. Hartley's body was taken to the Navigation Inn, Church, where Mr Hargreaves, coroner, held an inquest on Thursday. From his injuries, it seems that he was striking the drill with a hammer when the explosion happened. A steel drill was used in boring, contrary to the orders of the Government inspector, who some time ago recommended the use of a copper drill.*

Accrington Times, July 7th 1872:- *On Tuesday Mr Hargreaves, coroner, held an inquest at the Rose and Crown Inn, Oswaldtwistle, on Thomas Duxbury, collier, who was killed at Messrs Simpson's coal-pit at Aspen.*

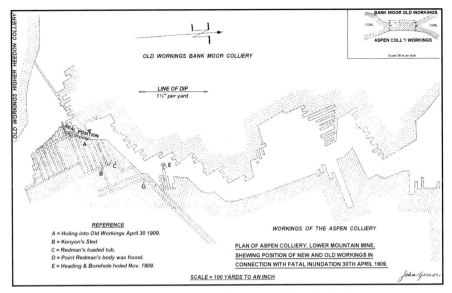

Fig. 2 The inundation of Aspen Colliery, April 30th 1909.

Bacup and Rossendale News, September 7th 1872:- *Thomas Duxbury, 12, of White Ash Lane, Oswaldtwistle, was found dead on Tuesday about 5.40 a.m. in the engine house at Aspen Colliery. He ought to have gone down the pit to work at 10.00 p.m. the previous evening, but instead seems to have gone into the engine house and fallen asleep under the machinery which is worked during the night. He was fearfully cut and bruised, apparently from injuries by the machine which caught him while still asleep.*

Accrington Times, August 8th 1891:- *A dataller named Thomas Yates, 59, of 9 Grove Street, Oswaldtwistle, was striking props at Aspen Colliery on Tuesday afternoon when a large piece of rock in the region of one ton fell upon his head, killing him on the spot. The inquest was at the Dog Inn, Oswaldtwistle, before Mr Robinson, coroner. Mr Dickinson, Inspector of Mines, was also present. John Taylor, collier, said he was working next to Yates when the rock fell. It was custom to move props when the colliers were working, and it was Yates' job to remove them. A verdict of Accidentally Killed was returned.*

On April 30th 1909 water from old workings inundated the mine. Twenty one men were underground and one, a 13 year old drawer named James Redmayne, was drowned. James Kenyon, a collier, gave evidence at the inquest. He told that he was at his work place when the water burst in, overtaking him and flooding the roadway. Struggling forwards with only 5 or 6 inches of air space between the water and roof, he came across James Redmayne, who was crying out in fear for his mother. Kenyon told the lad,

15

whose light had been extinguished, to stick close by him. Together they struggled forward yard by yard, till they were both thrown down by the force of the water. Further along, the force of the water threw Kenyon down again, and his lamp also went out. He was dazed, but, feeling something against his legs, was sure the lad was still with him. To his horror, when he reached down there was only a lump of shale being washed along with the water. Redmayne was found drowned many hours later, washed against the underground ginney. The rest of the men got out via the Town Bent Colliery Drift, which connected with the Aspen workings. The water was thought to have come from the abandoned Bank Moor Colliery. The incident was recorded in detail in the Mines Inspectors Reports for 1909.

Accrington Observer, February 1st 1902:- An inquest heard how Isaac Brindle, 42, of 16 New Lane, Oswaldtwistle, was killed while removing some props down Aspen Pit. The jury recorded a verdict of Accidental Death.

BACK O'TH' HEIGHT SD715214

The *List of Mines* for 1869 places this mine in Over Darwen, but that was probably Blacksnape Colliery, which was just south of Back o'th' Height, in the village of Blacksnape. It is marked on the 1848 OS Map and was being worked by John and Ralph Holden between 1854 and the early 1870s. A colliery named Back o'th' Height, including Green Height and Holden's, is listed in the *Catalogue of Abandoned Mines* in 1854. There is little evidence today of these pits, other than a number of overgrown mounds, which may be former spoil heaps or relics of field quarries, along the top side of Roman Road.

BANK MOOR SD722255

This early coal-pit lay 4 fields up Sough Lane from Four Lane Ends, on the left going to Belthorn, and is still marked as an air shaft on modern maps. Place, Anderton and Boardman originally worked the Upper Mountain Mine, but in the late 1830s it was taken over by Simpson and Rostron and Co. who sank shafts to the Lower Mountain Mine. According to the Mines Inspector's Report on an inundation at Aspen Colliery, Bank Moor was abandoned in 1856.

A number of reports tell that Simpson took orphans from the workhouse at Liverpool to work in his mines. Each child was given to a collier at the pit to work as his drawer in return for food and lodgings. The following is from the *Report on Child Labour in the Coal Mines:-*

Mr Whalley (Relieving Officer) says he had been in the habit of sending children from 7 to 9 years old from the workhouse to work in the coal pits, but had to take them back because they were so badly used. One Roger Taylor was sent by him to Bank Moor Colliery, where he stayed 12 months, there he was badly beaten. After 9 months he was brought back, and the doctor pronounced that he had been beaten so badly that he was not fit for

16

work. He was, notwithstanding, then sent to another colliery. He was not ill used there, but he died of smallpox. The ill usage is the beating of them with the pick handle.

The same report gave the following description of Bank Moor Colliery:-

The shaft is 36 yards deep. We were let down in wagons, which were wheeled onto a cage or flat plate of iron, kept in its horizontal position by iron brackets, and guided on its descent by iron rods, reaching from the top to the bottom of the shaft. These guide rods prevent the rope untwisting, as it is only a common round rope, about an inch and a quarter in diameter. A single horse is used to turn the wheel. Water oozes from the lower part of the shaft, and from the roof at the start of the runs, but, on the whole the place is dry, or rather just damp. The seam is 24 inches thick generally, in some runs it is in parts only 18 inches. The width is about 10 to 12 feet, with a flat and solid roof of stone, with no shale intervening between the good coal and the hard rock. The coal is drawn in wagons on iron rails. These wagons carry a load which requires two thrutchers. On the wagon on our run, there was a boy about 14, and a girl about 11. None of the children here draw by the belt. I was wheeled lying down on a low truck by the underlooker of the mine and an assistant, to the far end of the run, a distance of 90 yards. Here I saw the process of getting the coal. The getter was a youth of 16, who sat on the floor on a board. He made his blow from his right side to the left, horizontally, his head nearly touching the roof at every blow, though held rather reclining over his right shoulder. This posture must be an uneasy one until a person becomes accustomed to it. The thrutchers then filled the wagon, and pushed, or thrutched, it along the run, and I followed close to watch them.

The man who managed the machinery at the pit gave the following evidence:- *In the morning when the drawers go down, and also the getters, the horse is not at work, a man turns the wheel. Only one getter is allowed to go down at a time. Sometimes 3 (and always 2) drawers are are let down at once. The man's power is not sufficient for more.*

The following report illustrates the conditions endured by the children employed in the coal mines before the 1842 Act of Parliament.

Blackburn Standard. February 3rd 1841:- *An inquest was held last Friday at Lower Darwen on Ellen Whewell, 9, drawer at Simpson and Rostron's coalpit at Bank Moor, Oswaldtwistle, who died last Thursday. Last Monday she was drawing to the edge of the pit, when a piece of coal fell from a basket which was being hoisted up and struck her on the back. She worked for 3 more days, but on the 4th day she had to give up. A verdict of Accidental Death was recorded.*

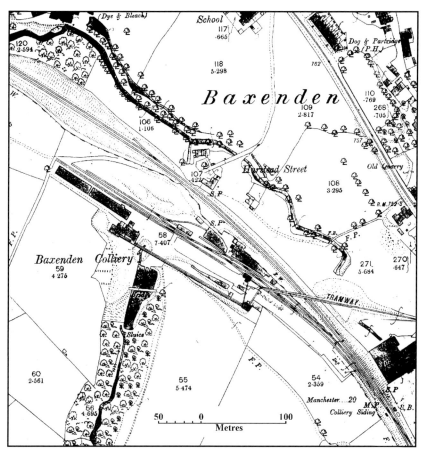

Fig. 3 Baxenden Colliery.

Mike Rothwell states that Bank Moor pit *"used a variety of winding devices, including hand winches, horse gins and steam engines"* and so the following might be a reference to the mine.[3]

Blackburn Standard, March 1841:- *An inquest was held last Saturday at the Britannia Tavern, Oswaldtwistle, on Thomas Edleston, 13, drawer in Simpson and Rostron's mine in Oswaldtwistle. Last Thursday he was being let down into the mine to work, when the rope of the whimsey slipped off about a yard. The basket went down about a yard, throwing him out. He fell to the bottom, a distance of about 28 yards. When taken up he was alive, but insensible, but died in about 20 minutes. His thighs appear to have been broken. Part of the shield which is fixed to the whimsey to keep the rope on had been broken off. The overlooker had told the carpenter to repair it, but he had neglected to do so. This seems to have caused the rope to slip, it being wet at the time. Accidental Death was recorded.*

18

Blackburn Standard, July 5th 1843:- *An explosion took place at the Left Engine Pit in Oswaldtwistle on Monday about 7 o'clock by which Edmund Aspden, drawer, died. He and 2 other lads went up to the pithead with a lighted candle, and the foul air became ignited and exploded. The 2 other lads got to the pit eye but were severely burnt. It is thought that Aspden missed the direction in trying to return. The pit belongs to Sir Robert Peel, and is worked by Messrs Simpson and Rostron.*

Blackburn Standard, June 26th 1844:- *John Hargreaves, coroner, held an inquest at Oswaldtwistle last Wednesday on Thomas Lomax, 16, drawer for James Hindle, a collier in Simpson and Rostron's coalmine. On Easter Tuesday last Lomax was sitting down, when he should have been at work. When Hindle asked him why he was not working he got no reply, so he struck him with his hand on the right side. Lomax began to cry, but continued his work all day. When he got home in the evening he complained of pain at the bottom of his stomach but did not say he had been hit. He was ill for a month and was taken to Mr Grime, surgeon, who ordered leeches and a blister. But Lomax got worse and died. An examination then revealed inflammation on the right side caused by a blow or a fall. The jury brought the verdict of Manslaughter against James Hindle.*

BAXENDEN PIT (OLD)   SD769269

Although coal-pits were worked at Baxenden before 1800, the real exploitation of the coal seams began with the arrival of the railway branch line in the late 1840s when Railway Pit was developed. Before this, coal was mined by small drifts and shallow shafts, on which little information is available. A number of shafts were sunk along the line of Manchester Road, and these are shown on the 1844 OS Map. The coal workings around this area date from at least the 1820s, as shown by the following report, which gives us some details about early mining at Baxenden, but unfortunately not the name of the pit involved.

Blackburn Mail, November 15th 1826:- *A most gross act of mischief was perpetrated at a colliery at Baxenden a few days ago. The colliers arrived at the pit and, as one of them was about to descend, discovered that the rope holding the basket was nearly cut through. Had it not been for this most fortunate discovery, the first man who attempted to descend would in all probability have been dashed to pieces. Not the slightest knowledge has transpired as to who the villains are who committed this act.*

Ventilation of pits at this time was rudimentary or even non-existent. In its most basic form, a fire would be lit at the bottom of a shaft to create a draught as the warm air rose up the shaft, but this was very dangerous at gassy mines. Other methods included throwing water down the shaft, which to some extent dispersed the air and cleansed the workings. Coal was got by hand using picks and shovels, and was extracted leaving pillars of unworked coal to support the roof. These pillars were often removed immediately before the abandonment of a pit. Workings rarely extended many yards, owing to ventilation and haulage problems. Instead, new shafts were sunk close by and the process repeated.

Rossendale Free Press, October 14th 1893:- *John Towers, 26, of Worsley Street, Accrington, was killed in a roof fall at Baxenden Colliery on Monday. At the inquest held at Accrington on Wednesday, Mr Gerrard, Inspector of Mines, was present, and Mr H.H. Bolton represented the colliery company. They heard that at about 11.15 a.m. on Monday, Towers was pulling down some props in No.5 drift. The roof was supported by the props, and Towers had taken some 30 or 40 props for a distance of about 10 yards when Heap, the day man who was working about 10 yards away, heard a groan and turned to see Towers face down on the ground with a large stone weighing about 2 tons on his head. Heap gave the alarm and got help, and Towers was released in 10 or 15 minutes. He appeared to be dead. Heap said it was usual to take down the props, but he could not account for the falling of the stone. Shortly before it fell, they had reduced the roof supports to some 6 or 7 props. The jury was told that Towers had worked in the pits since he was 12 years old. They returned a verdict of Accidental Death.*

BELTHORN   SD723246
Situated beside the B6232, due east of Belthorn Village, remains at this colliery include the raised pit bank of the Bye Pit – a name given to a pit which was on higher ground than the main winding shaft, usually to promote natural ventilation - colliery spoil and a number of engine beds. A capped shaft can be seen at Eden Pit (SD720248) which was worked in connection with Belthorn Colliery.

Thomas Tattersall sank the pit in the early 1800s, and George Yates took over in the 1840s. He also owned Duckworth Hill Colliery and there are a number of reports of abuse of the children he employed underground. William Forrest, 15, said in 1842 that at George Yates' he was caught in the side with a pick handle by Joseph Eccles, and it knocked him over. He was sick and had to be taken out of the pit, and was off work for 3 days. He added that he got 5 shillings a week wages, which he gave to his aunt, who gave him plenty of meat. Joseph Waring, 10, said that he worked at George Yates' Colliery, which was so wet that the men sat on a board when they worked and laded out the water every half hour. He added that sometimes he drew with a belt, and was obliged to stoop or else walk with his hands. Other times he strouched and this was the hardest work. Billy Bobby Yeates (the man he worked for) sometimes got him to the end of the run, and beat him with the pick handle or a stick because he was not strong enough to draw as much as the others. Joseph stayed at Yates' colliery for half a year, then, when he got ill from being beaten, he was sent back to the workhouse.

Simpson and Young acquired the colliery around 1853. They sank the shafts to the Lower Mountain Mine and also sank the Bye Pit. The colliery,

PLATE III Raised Pit Bank at Belthorn Bye Pit (J. Nadin).

abandoned in 1884, also had a drift entrance near Wood Head Farm, west of Belthorn village. Another Belthorn pit was William Henry Shaw's mine in Yate and Pickup Bank which worked the Upper Mountain Mine and fireclay and was abandoned in May 1901. An aerial ropeway took fireclay down to Whitebirk Glazed Brickworks. In the mid 1890s, John Bury was the manager and the pit had 33 men underground and 7 on the surface. A small area of Lower Mountain Mine was worked by George Hargreaves and Co. from drift workings near Bank Fold, south of Belthorn village. This was listed in *The Collieries of Lancashire in 1879*, but was abandoned by the mid 1880s. In 1991, fears were expressed that low level nuclear waste had been dumped down shafts at Belthorn pits during 1951 and 1952.

Blackburn Newspaper, May 29th 1811:- *To be let for a term of years, at the New Inn Blackburn a valuable coal mine and bed of coal within the township of Oswaldtwistle. These mines, lately rented by Thomas Tattersall, are now held by Mr John Tattersall and Sons.*

Darwen News, June 1st 1898:- *On Saturday Mr Robinson, coroner, held an inquest at the Dog Inn, Yate and Pickup Bank, on George Nuttall, 52, of 6 James Street, Belthorn, who was killed on Friday at Messrs W.H. Shaw and Co's colliery, Yate and Pickup Bank. He was blasting there when the roof of the workings gave way. The jury returned a verdict of Accidental Death.*

Accrington Gazette, April 16th 1904:- *Cr Duckworth said the screen which the owners of the aerial ropeway from Belthorn to Knuzden had promised to erect over the highway had not been constructed. The surveyor replied that the owners had promised to push the work forward.*

Accrington Observer, May 4th 1910:- *Ephrain Armitage, collier, of Belthorn was killed by a roof fall at Messrs Shaw's Drift Pit, Waterside. He was found by the manager, John Bury. Inquest heard how 9 feet of roof was unsupported, when according to the Coal Mines Act the roof should be propped every 4 feet.*

BLACK MOSS   SD783274
The 210 feet deep shaft at Black Moss was in the fields behind Baxenden House and was an air and secondary access shaft for Hole in the Bank and Railway Pits. There was machinery there, but whether it was for winding men and materials, pumping or both is difficult to tell. The following, apparently malicious, incident took place during the 1873 miners' strike.

Accrington Times, February 22nd 1873:- *On Wednesday morning Henry Spencer, the engineer, discovered a fire at the engine house at Messrs George Hargreaves and Co's Black Moss Pit. The building was a temporary one built of wood and burned fiercely. It is supposed to be the work of an incendiary, and the proprietors have offered a reward about the same.*

Although the following report states Black Moor coal pit, it is probably the Black Moss Shaft.

Bacup and Rossendale Times, December 5th 1874:- *Richard Hindle, 17, an engine tenter at Messrs Ashworth and Hargreaves and Co's Black Moor pit, Baxenden, died on Sunday from injuries received on November 24th, when he tried to start his engine by stepping on the spokes of the flywheel. This sudden impetus did not give him time to withdraw his leg, which was so badly crushed between the flywheel and engine that it had to be amputated.*

Accrington Times, March 15th 1884:- *An inquest was held on Monday at the Railway Hotel, Baxenden, on John Woods Lambert, 14, son of Thomas and Sarah Lambert of Crow Street, Baxenden, and formerly of Bury. On Sunday March 2nd, after his dinner, he went for a walk with his brother William, 17. They were joined by Thomas Chadwick and Thomas Alston, and they rambled on Pen Moss and Black Moss. The others wished him to return, and when he left them he made towards home, but he never got there. The police were informed, and notices were issued, but for a week there was no news of him. On Saturday afternoon, Mr George Smith, undermanager at Baxenden Collieries, with Thomas Beckett, miner, were examining the workings and, when they went to the air shaft, they found Lambert's mangled body on the floor. An examination on the surface by PC Jennings showed marks on the 8 feet high wall surrounding the pit mouth, which is in a field* behind Baxenden House. There were foot marks as if someone had climbed the wall, and a few coping stones were missing. It is thought the youth climbed to the top, and was sitting on the coping stones when they gave way, plunging him down the mine. Mr Dickinson, Inspector of Mines, was at the inquest.

BLACKSNAPE   SD710214

There are a number of shafts and old coal pits close to the east side of Roman Road in Blacksnape Village. The 1848 OS Map shows 6 old coal pits and 4 coal pits, which were still working. The following reference to one of Messrs Place's pits may be to Hattons or Blacksnape, which were both worked by Place before Hoddlesden was sunk.

Manchester Guardian, March 5th 1853:- *Last Thursday an inquest was held at Over Darwen on Thomas Isherwood, 18, drawer in Messrs Place's coal pit, Over Darwen. On the previous Thursday, he came up the pit in a loaded basket of coal, but, instead of the basket stopping at the usual place, it was carried much higher. As a result, the pulley broke and the rope slipped off, throwing the basket and its occupant down the pit. Isherwood was dashed at the bottom, and killed on the spot. One of the pit's owners, and several other witnesses said that the engineer, Richard Woodcock, was to blame for not being at his proper post and paying due attention to the arrival of the basket at the top of the pit. The jury returned a verdict of manslaughter against the engineer.*

BRANDWOODS'   SD703225

Marked on the 1848 OS Map, this mine dates from the start of the 19th century and was worked by Henry Sudell, a Blackburn merchant, who also worked other pits locally. Sudell Road was named after him and originally ended near the pit. His enterprise failed, however, and the pits passed into the hands of John and William Brandwood. The mines were abandoned by the 1890s. No remains of Brandwoods' Pit have survived and the area is now built up by Rose Street, Two Gates Drive etc. Later workings took place at Ellison Fold.

BROADFIELD   SD749269

Place, Anderson and Boardman worked this mine before 1840. They were followed by Simpson and Young in 1854, and the Thomas Simpson Co. in 1869.[4] Mike Rothwell tells us that Simpson sank a new shaft 191 feet to the Lower Mountain Mine in 1848.[2] This seam was abandoned in 1892. As workings progressed, a second winding shaft was sunk at White Syke (SD747252) and coke ovens were erected just off Fielding Lane. In 1871 W. and J. Yates rebuilt and enlarged the winding engine. The 1848 shaft is marked by a capped shaft marker in the field almost opposite the junction of Broadfield with Pothouse Lane, at Oswaldtwistle. Some of the colliery's output was delivered to Moscow Mills by tramroad, and the stone setts can still be seen in the mill yard.

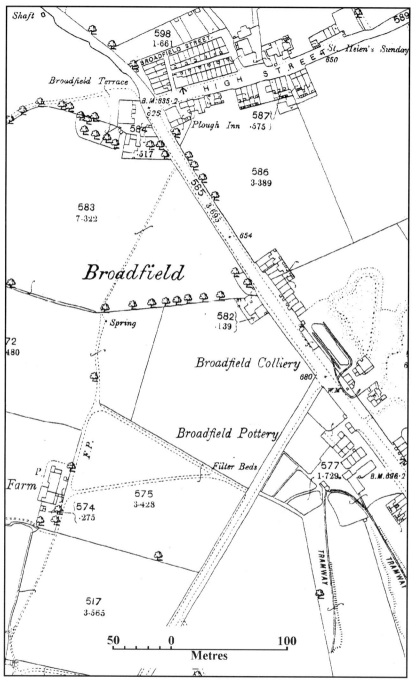

Fig. 4 Broadfield Colliery.

24

Accrington Times, October 19th 1872:- *Mr Hargreaves, coroner, held an inquest at the Sough Inn on John Aspin, 24, who worked at Messrs Thomas Simpson and Co's colliery on Broadfield Moor. On Tuesday James Yates, underlooker, was pointing out some work which would have to be done on the morrow, near some pillars. Without any warning, a huge stone fell, bringing down a portion of rough stuff with it and burying Aspin beneath it. Yates escaped with slight injuries. A verdict of Accidental Death was recorded. Aspin leaves a wife and 3 or 4 little children.*

Accrington Times, February 1st 1873:- *On Thursday, Richard Wolstenholme, 35, miner at Messrs Simpson and Company's Broadfield Pit, was getting pillars, when a large stone fell on him without warning and he was killed instantly. A number of his fellow workers recovered his body. He leaves a widow, for whom much sympathy will be felt as she is near her confinement, and one child. The inquest will be held today.*

Blackburn Times, October 12th 1872:- *An apparently destitute and aged man entered Mrs Bennett's cook shop in Abbey Street, Accrington, on Thursday week asking for alms. He told her he was a poor old collier and he had a wife and 3 children to support. He added that he was forced to go from door to door begging. She asked if the parish would do anything for him and he said no, as General Scarlet left him half a crown a week when he died. Just then PC Lord entered, for he had been an unknown listener, and said, "That will do, Jack. Come with me". The poor old collier knew his man and bobbled to the door, his lameness deserting him. Called John Wilkinson, he has been on the road for 16 years. He was brought before Mr Grimshaw on Tuesday, and sent to gaol for a month.*

Blackburn Times, December 29th 1883:- *A collier named Thomas Ince (?) of Green Haworth, working at Messrs Thomas Simpson's Broadfield Colliery was working in the pit last week when the roof gave way, and he sustained serious back injuries.*

BROAD OAK   SD772276
The site of this pit is found by going down Broad Oak Road, just above the police and fire station on Manchester Road, Accrington. Follow the road through the former Broad Oak Print Works, now a foam manufacturers. This is a public right of way to Laund Farm and a network of paths in this area. The tarmac road wends to the right and left, then becomes a rough track. Ignoring the track on the right, bear slightly left to a pair of steel gates on the right. This is the site of Broad Oak Colliery. It is on private land, but a large area of colliery waste and the foundations of a number of small buildings can be seen through the gates. The stone embankment on the right is a brick-lined tunnel with a concrete top. In a direct line with the old Tag Clough Pit, it was probably used for hauling coal from there for distribution at Broad Oak pit top.

The original Broad Oak Colliery, or Broad Oak No.1, must date from around 1880, as it is not mentioned in *The Collieries of Lancashire in 1879*. It worked the Lower Mountain Mine, said to be 2 foot thick. Both Broad Oak Colliery and Tag Clough are in the 1896 *List of Mines*, when Nathan Haworth was the manager and both pits employed 62 miners and 9 surface workers. According to the *Catalogue of Plans of Abandoned Mines*, Broad Oak No.2 worked an area around the old Laund Pit Colliery and was abandoned in 1939. However, the pit is mentioned in the *List of Mines* for 1940.

There is no trace of what was probably a cupola shaft marked just above the Broad Oak mouthing on the1893 OS map. A furnace placed at the bottom of this shaft would create a draught, bringing fresh air into the workings. Stopping, or air doors, at the entrance to one of the drifts forced the air to take the long route around the workings via the other drift mouth. The closure of Broad Oak Colliery in 1939 ended a long tradition of coal extraction in this area.

BROCKLEHEAD   SD706230
Brocklehead colliery, from the early 1840s, was NW of Brocklehead Farm off Roman Road. Pits, including Brocklehead Colliery, are marked on the 1848 OS Map as 2 coal pits and 2 old coal pits. Areas of disturbed ground here indicate former mining activity.

BROOKSIDE   SD727272
Coal mining at Brookside dates from around the turn of the 19th century. James Reddish, a calico cloth printer of Brookside Printworks, took over the colliery in 1818 to supply the printworks with fuel. Around 70 men were employed here at this time, working the Upper Mountain Mine.[2] In the 1860s the pit was worked by a partnership of Reddish and Bickham, followed by Thomas Simpson and Co The pit was abandoned shortly after 1886, when the last fatality was recorded. The following accident, although recorded as Brookhouse Pit, was more than likely at Brookside.

Accrington Times, August 4th 1860:- *An inquest was held on Monday at the Guide public house, Darwen, on John Sharples, 58, engine tenter, of Lower Darwen, who was killed at Messrs Reddish and Bickham's Brookside Collery, near Blackburn, on Friday, July 27th. Henry Ashworth, banksman, of Cabin End, Oswaldtwistle, said that Sharples started as engine tenter at the pit on the previous Thursday morning, but had been employed in a similar capacity for the last 20 years at other places, and was also employed at that pit when it was being sunk. On Friday about 4.00 p.m., as there were no coals ready to be wound up, Sharples preferred to pump some water. To do that he had to disconnect the engine from the winding apparatus and connect it with the pumping apparatus. To place the winding apparatus out of gear it is necessary after turning off the steam to move a sliding pedestal with a crow bar. This was Sharples' duty, but, as he was not strong enough, Ashworth did it for him. Then Sharples leaned through the flywheel to place a small*

26

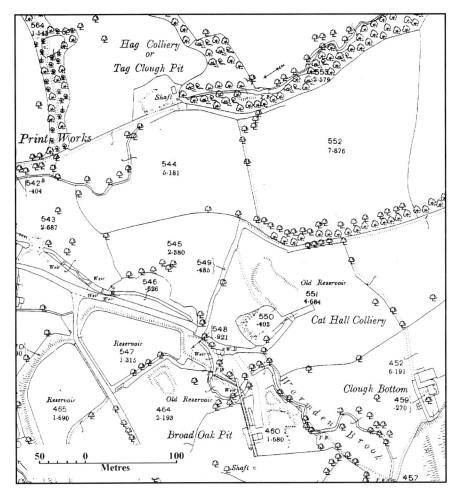

Fig. 5 Cat Hall, Broad Oak and Tag Clough Pits.

*plug of wood, or stop bit, between the fast pedestal to prevent it moving
backwards and reconnecting the engine with the winding apparatus. While
Sharples was putting the stop bit in, the flywheel moved and one of its arms
caught him on the back of the head, crushing him against the pedestal hole
and flinging him face down into the wheel race. The wheel moved because
he had not effectually shut off the steam, and the valve was not perfectly
closed. He died 10 minutes after he was removed from the wheel race. John
Holden, mechanic at Brookside Print Works, said he attended the colliery
engine when it was out of order. He also thought it likely that Sharples had
left some steam in the valve. He added that the inspector of mines viewed
the machinery that morning, and they had devised a scheme to prevent the
necessity of leaning through the flywheel when putting in a stop bit. The*

27

engine tenter was able to ascertain whether the steam was shut off effectually, and Sharples was wanting in care in not having done so before leaning through the flywheel. Thomas Sharples said the deceased was his brother. William Holden said there were 2 wounds to John Sharples' head and a small hole in his left temple. The jury returned a verdict of Accidentally Killed.

The following accident, recorded as at Brookhouse Pit, was also more than likely at Brookside.

Accrington Times, September 26th 1874:- Mr Hargreaves, coroner, held an inquest on Monday at the Knuzden Brook Inn on James Kelly, 15, of Kitchen Row, Oswaldtwistle, a drawer at Messrs Simpson and Company's Brookhouse Pit. On Friday morning he went down the pit in his usual health with some other youths, but on arriving at the bottom he fell over a sledge. Shortly afterwards he exclaimed, "Oh my back!" and became senseless. He was carried to the engine house on the pit bank, but died within a few minutes. The jury returned the verdict that the deceased died suddenly in the pit, and there was not sufficient evidence to show the cause.

Accrington Times, May 18th 1878:- In consequence of the strike in the cotton industry, Messrs Simpson have given notice to their colliers at Brookside Pit to work short time. The employers want the men to work half time each day, and the men wish to work a day and play a day. The employers would not consent to this, and on Tuesday morning the men turned out. Between nine and ten they met around the Black Dog at the higher end of Oswaldtwistle, then marched down Union Road followed by a large crowd which increased as they progressed. On the road some of the men entered shops where food was sold and demanded loaves, bacon, sausages etc. from the shopkeepers. It is said they took them forcibly if the shopkeepers refused to give them to them. Rather than have any trouble, the shopkeepers gave the articles, and the men said they were for those suffering from the strike. They marched on as far as the Castle Inn, laden by this time with articles of every description. A halt was made near the Commercial Mill, and it looked as though some disturbance would be created, but the constables assisted by a number of spinners dispersed the crowd, and the colliers returned up Union Road.

BURTON   SD699216
This pit was near Turncroft Road, Darwen. It and the Mill Pit (not the one belonging to the Hiltons of old Darwen Paper Mills) are marked on the 1844 OS Map. An engine house nearby suggests motive power.

CAT HOLE   SD772277
This mine, whose name is said to have come from the wild cats which roamed the area, has been extensively landscaped and little now remains. The site was NW of Clough Bottom Farm, almost facing Broad Oak Colliery, and traces of a reservoir can be made out. The pit was one of Accrington's oldest

collieries, dating from at least 1820, and consisted of drift workings driven
into the hillside to work the Lower Mountain Mine. It is noted in the *List of
Mines* for 1869 and 1879 as being worked by George Hargreaves and Co.,
but before this it was worked by Hargreaves, Ashworth and Co. Cat Hole
Colliery was abandoned in 1891, when its workings were merged with the
nearby Broad Oak Colliery.

Blackburn Standard, January 13th 1847:- *On Monday afternoon last, James
Haworth was killed in a coal pit a little above the Broad Oaks Works, near
Accrington. As he removed a prop, the earth fell in on him, crushing him
dreadfully. He left a wife to deplore his death.*

Burnley Advertiser, January 28th 1860:- *The men in the employ of
Hargreaves, Ashworth and Co. struck on Tuesday morning and resolved
not to return until they had an advance in wages. This resolution was come
to with an overwhelming majority at a meeting of the pitmen at the Queen's
Hotel, Accrington, on Monday night. The reason for the strike is that, if
they continue to work until the expiration of their contract which would be
in March, then their employer would not require the same quantity of coal
as they require at present, when there is not a load beforehand at the pithead.
In order to secure better terms they have run the risk of striking without
giving notice. Four pits are on strike.*

Accrington Times, August 4th 1860:- *Mr J. Hargreaves, coroner, held an
inquest at the Bay Horse Inn, Baxenden on the 27th instant, on James Smith,
41, collier, who was severely burnt in the Cat Hole Pit on Thursday the
17th. ult. Mr Dickinson, inspector of mines, was present and Mr Pickop of
Blackburn appeared on behalf of Messrs Hargreaves, Ashworth and Co.
James Smith, of Baxenden, said the deceased was his son. He was married
with 2 children and had worked in coal mines since he was 9 years old.
James Taylor, collier, of New Accrington, said he worked with James Smith.
On the morning of the 17th, he was working 200 yards from Smith who was
getting coal. Smith and John Entwistle were working as usual, when Taylor
suddenly heard a great noise. He went to the place where the noise had
come from, and found Smith on his knees. Smith asked Taylor to find his
clothes and appeared to be burnt. He also asked him why he had not been
sharper. Nothing else was said. Taylor then told a juryman that they had
worked with naked candles for the last 4 years, while he had been engaged
there. The colliery had been worked for the last 20 years, and they had
never found it necessary to use lamps. John Entwistle, collier, of Baxenden,
said he was working with Smith on the 17th and they were using iron picks
when he heard a great noise and his light was blown out. He then made his
way to his clothes, and as he was making his way out to the pit mouth he
found Smith in the way kneeling. Smith told him that he was burnt and said he
had made a hole in another place, and left with his candle. He then returned
without a light and made the hole bigger, and when he took the light to the
hole it fired. The hole entered into another work, where a man had been*

29

engaged about a fortnight ago, with naked light. Entwistle told the inspector that about 30 minutes before the explosion, his candle blazed up, and there was a dark appearance at the top of it for a minute or two, but he did not know what this indicated. He heard from his gaffer, Henry Pilkington, that there was a bit of firedamp in the place, and the latter told him the day before the explosion, while he was making his rounds, to be cautious, but Entwistle did not understand what was meant. Smith was not present at the time. They had a little explosion in the pit a fortnight last Monday. In the same part of the pit where the present explosion happened a man named George Taylor was burnt. Between these two explosions, no order was given to him not to use naked lights. Entwistle had received a rule book, but could not read it, and it had not been read to him. He told Mr Pickop that, since George Taylor's accident, the cracks had been plastered up in the pit. He had never noticed firedamp in the pit himself. Henry Pilkington, underlooker, of Wood Nook, New Accrington, said he had been in his present situation 18 years. He never knew of sulphur in the mine before George Taylor was burnt on the 9th. ult. No work was carried on until the 16th inst. and he intended the work should have stood until the 21st. When Pilkington discovered Smith making the hole, he told him that the work ought to stop until they got the air gates right. Smith said he was not very well, and it was easier to work there. Pilkington asked him if he was accustomed to sulphur, and Smith said he was. Pilkington told him that, when he had made the hole, he must leave it and go back to his own work until Pilkington came again. Pilkington said he had worked in coal pits over 40 years, and never saw the necessity for lamps. He had gone with Thomas Hindle on Tuesday last into the pit, and found sulphur in 4 or 5 different places. He intended to remedy this by sinking an air shaft, and that portion should not be worked until they got good air. He told the inspector that the roof had fallen where Taylor worked, since the accident. Although he found sulphur in the works, he did not order safety lamps to be used. According to the rules, safety lamps ought to have been used. Mr Dickinson said he had examined the works that morning, and it would not be safe to work in it with either lamps or candles. The coroner said that, although there was no doubt but Smith met his death through his own carelessness, he thought Henry Pilkington was also to be blamed for not stopping the work in that portion of the pit where he discovered sulphur. Mr Dickinson said that when the air shaft was opened up, it would be safe to work in the pit either with naked lights or lamps, but he would report the case to the Secretary of State, as he thought Henry Pilkington was to blame, for not seeing the 31st law put into force. The jury returned a verdict of Accidental Death.

Accrington Times, January 5th 1867:- *Last Thursday, John Entwistle, miner, of Fig Pie Hall, was working at Cat Hall Pit when a quantity of stone and rubble fell from the roof and buried him. He called for help and assistance was immediately given by the drawer and two colliers. He was taken home and medical assistance was called in. His back and shoulders were badly bruised, but no bones broken or dislocated, and he is making good progress.*

Accrington Times, July 11th 1868:- *On Saturday Mr Hargreaves, coroner, held an inquest at the Bay Horse Inn, Baxenden, on Peter Parker, 26, miner, of Baxenden. Mr Dickinson, Inspector of Mines, and Mr Bolton, manager for Messrs Hargreaves, Ashworth and Co., were present. Owing to the severe injuries received by Richard Hoyle, who was working with Parker at the time, his medical adviser requested him not to leave the house. In consequence, the coroner and the jury had to go to the witness's house, where Richard Hoyle told them that he was working with Parker in Cat Hall pit last Thursday about noon. They had drilled a hole in the rock underneath the coal for blasting it. Parker put in 5 charges full of powder. Hoyle gave him some hay to put in after the powder. They then put up the spindle, and after that Parker put in some dirt. Parker held an iron rammer, and Hoyle struck it with a hammer, perhaps 6 times, when the powder exploded. He believed Parker was killed instantly. John Rushton and others came to their assistance. They had no copper rammers, or wooden ones, and were working as normal. He and Parker were partners, and did this work by the yard. Ann Parker, Peter Parker's widow, said he had left her with a child aged 8 months. John Rushton, collier, of New Accrington, said he went to Parker after the explosion. He assisted in removing his body from the pit, and also laid it out. The left arm was smashed below the elbow, and his right arm was burnt. His lip was nearly cut in two, and his teeth and gums broken. George Smith, underviewer, said he was at the place about 20 minutes before the explosion. He thought Parker had not got the powder in the far end of the hole, but he said nothing as Parker had 10 or 11 years' experience. The cause of the explosion might be some loose powder in the hole. Mr Dickinson said the use of an iron rammer to get the wadding on to the powder was the only way of proceeding. Smith said he had not seen a circular letter against using an iron rammer. Mr Bolton, manager, said he did not remember receiving a circular. Mr Dickinson said he sent half a dozen, and expected they would be distributed among the colliers. Mr Bolton said that the recommendation in the circular might be necessary when stone was being blasted, but Parker was blasting shale. Mr Dickinson said that there were about 8 men killed last year owing to the same cause. The men should not use an iron rammer, until the wadding is near the powder. The witness said the rammer had been used in this way since he could remember, and no accident ever occurred. Mr Dickinson said that might be so, but the experience of a wide district ought to be taken. If the hint he gave in the circular had been adopted, the man's life might have been saved. The coroner summed up, remarking that no blame should be attached to anyone. The jury returned a verdict of Accidental Death, recommending that the suggestion made by Mr Dickinson be carried out. Mr Bolton promised to see that it was.*

Accrington Times, September 24th 1870:- *Yesterday Mr H.U. Hargreaves, coroner, held an inquest at the Bay Horse Inn, Baxenden on Matthew Smith, 28, who was killed in Cathall pit on Tuesday when he fell about 12 yards from the top of a shaft in the workings to the bottom. Mr Dickinson, Inspector of Mines, was present. The first witness was John Smith of Baxenden, brother of the deceased and a labourer at Cathall pit. He was at the pit and saw his brother when he was at the bottom. Two men and 2 boys were on the front of the shaft. A lurry, or moving platform, was on the shaft top, and they were about to push it back when he fell down. The witness was standing with his back to his brother when he fell. He did not know the cause of his falling, except that he, perhaps, might have slipped. He lived until 2 o'clock the next morning. George Kenyon, collier, of Baxenden said he saw Smith fall as he was walking on the outside of the shaft, but in the pit. Mr Dickinson explained that there was a level from the surface, and that Smith was walking on the level. The shaft referred to went from one level to another. Kenyon added that, as he was about to put the lurry over the shaft top, he saw Smith put his foot on the foreside and fall down. Smith had been blasting with him on the lower level, but at the time of the accident was walking across the level. Cross-examined by the Inspector, Kenyon added that Smith stood there until he had pulled the wagon off and wound him up the shaft with the windlass. Smith was quite conversant with the arrangement of the pit. Kenyon's candle was stuck on the side of a wagon and there were 2 or 3 yards of space to pass in. Smith need not have been so near the shaft, which was about 2 yards wide. Mr Ormerod, the foreman, said he and Smith lodged together in America and, during the 7 weeks since their return, Smith had complained that if he did not sit down he would fall. Ormerod added that he had been told that Smith's wife, knowing he was subject to dizziness, told him to get a boy to assist him at his work. Richard Harrison, colliery manager, said that the shaft was about 1,200 yards from the mouth of Cathall level. Called No.3 shaft, it was about 12 yards high. The top of the shaft was in the middle of a 9 foot 6 inch working or bord, with a space of 9 inches round the side of the windlass. He had gone there the next morning, and could not see how Smith missed his footing. He thought he must have felt faint. Only 2 sides of the shaft were open, and on each of them there was a hand rail 3ft 3in from the ground. The other 2 sides were boarded up. A verdict of Accidental Death was returned.*

Accrington Times, December 16th 1871:- On Thursday afternoon, two young miners, John Crabb and James Birch, were seriously injured in an explosion at Cat Hall Colliery. They were driving down a drift, and needed to blast the roof. They drilled the hole and put in some gunpowder and were ramming the charge home when the shot fired. Both men were close to the drill hole and appear to have been struck by the rammer, suffering burns and bruising. Crabb's left hand is so badly injured that the first finger had to be amputated by Dr Russell, who is attending both men. His eyes are also injured and his face burnt. Birch is much more injured. The front of his head was laid open, and had to be stitched together, and it is feared he will lose his sight. His chest is also injured. Both men are at Mr Grimshaw's beerhouse, Chapel Street, where they lodged. They had copper protection for the rammers, but whether they were in use at the time is another question. Probably the iron came into contact with the roof and struck a spark which caused the explosion.

Accrington Times, September 28th 1872:- *On Saturday morning at 3 o'clock many of Accrington's inhabitants were awakened by the fire-bell. Rain was pouring down, but this did not stop a large number of people rushing out to see where the fire was. It was in the vicinity of Broad Oak Print Works, but in a wooden shed on the bank at Cat Hall colliery. The fire engine was taken out, but stopped before it reached the spot, as the wooden hut used for joinery and smithy purposes had been entirely consumed. The flames were put out by buckets of water shortly after assistance arrived. The damage will be about £30.*

Accrington Observer, July 17th 1897:- *The inquest on John Hamer, 15, son of William Henry Hamer, engineer, of 3 Devonshire street, Accrington, was resumed in the court room of the Town Hall on Wednesday afternoon before Mr Robinson. There was some doubt whether the boy died from the effects of an accident at Cathall Pit, where he was employed, or from natural causes, and the case had been adjourned so that further evidence could be procured. Mr R. Kidd Whittaker appeared for the accident club connected with the pit, and Mr J. Sharples for the deceased. Mr Gerrard, Inspector of Mines, was also present. It was alleged that Hamer met with an accident at the pit on September 18th 1896, but resumed work shortly afterwards. It was also affirmed that in November or December he had a second accident at the pit. Mary Ann Greenwood, wife of Ernest Greenwood, 3 Devonshire Street, and Hamer's sister, said she took him to the dentist to have a tooth drawn over 12 months ago. She could only see the dentist's wife, Mrs Thompson, who broke the tooth while trying to pull it and told the boy to come again the next day, but he did not go because the tooth stopped aching. She paid 6d. for the operation. DS Garvey spoke to Mrs Thompson about the case, but she could not recollect anything about it and he did not consider it of any use to bring her as a witness. James Anderson, Back Manchester Road, who had worked as a drawer at Cathall pit a little over 6 months ago, said Hamer was drawing an empty tub when he ran into a prop and, slipping on the ground, fell on the side of his face. The blow he received was a hard one and he said he was knocked sick. His face was swollen and, on the day after the accident, he drew 2 or 3 tubs less than his usual number on account of being unwell. Two weeks afterwards he went on the sick. Mr Whittaker said Hamer had a swollen neck after the accident, but none before, and the injury he received was on the left temple close to the eye. William Henry Grumm, drawer, of Lorne Farm, said he remembered his own and Hamer's tubs colliding before last hay time, when Hamer's tub hit him on the eye. Richard Whittaker, engine tenter and secretary of the Collier's Accident and Burial Club, of 1 Mansion Street, said he could not remember Hamer being on the club in June of last year, but there was a record of an injury to him on June 6th 1897, and it was decided on the 12th to grant him accident pay starting 3 days from receiving his doctor's paper. Hamer received 5 weeks' pay. Nathan Haworth, colliery manager, of 43 Carter Street, said he first heard of an accident to Hamer on December 10th 1896. There was no claim made on them for wages or anything else that he knew of, and it* was not until about a fortnight ago that the lad's father went to the pit, and said he had been hurt there. Haworth said he did not think Hamer had been hurt at the pit. The drawers occasionally received bumps, but he had never known a boy to stay off work on that account. Dr Nuttall said he and his assistant first saw Hamer on December 21st 1896. He had a swelling of the left side of his face, and his lower jaw was fixed, which Dr Nuttall concluded was the result of an accident, which had probably fractured the upper part of his lower jaw. Mr Nathan Smith, secretary of Blackburn Infirmary, said Hamer was treated there on December 31st for an enlarged gland. On February 4th he was taken in as an in-patient and was operated on for a tubercular gland in the neck. After being discharged on March 3rd, he was treated as an out-patient. Dr Holmes, assistant to Dr Clayton, said he saw Hamer on June 10th when he diagnosed a hopeless case of tuberculosis, which he thought had caused the swelling. Dr Geddie said it was highly probable there had been a fracture of the jaw, but he attributed Hamer's condition to the disease. Dr Cooper said the lad's death was entirely the result of an accident, the jaw having been fractured but not set. The coroner said that there was no doubt that Hamer had received a knock about June last year, but they had nothing definite about it. He was evidently a tubercolous subject, and the only verdict which they could return was that he had died from a tumour of the face, which might have been caused by an injury. The jury gave the verdict that death was due to exhaustion resulting from a tumour of the face probably due to an injury received while at work as a drawer at Cathall Pit about 9 months ago.

Accrington Gazette, December 25th 1909:- Mr Robinson, coroner, held an inquest on Wednesday at Baxenden Liberal Club, on John Taylor, 21, coal miner, of 2 Hill Street, Baxenden, who died as a result of a scratch received whilst working at Cat Hall Pit. Jane Shorrock said he was her nephew and lived with her. He came home on Saturday week, and said he had scratched his wrist whilst filling the wagon and levelling the coal with his hand. It looked like a cut on the inside of his wrist and was not wrapped up when he came home. She washed it for him, and got it as clean as she could. He went to Accrington in the evening. He did not put anything on it, and made no complaint that night. Next morning he had a lump under his arm, and he complained of pain. Dr Peterson of Oswaldtwistle attended him, and he died at 6.15 p.m. last Monday. Dr Peterson said he saw Taylor on Monday, and found he was suffering from acute blood poisoning, which resulted in death. There was no inflammation in the wound on the wrist, but there was a faint red line up the middle of his arm from it and there was no doubt the scratch was the cause of the blood poisoning. The jury found that Taylor accidentally came to his death.

CHADWICK   SD771266

Marked as Colliery on the 1848 map, this pit probably gave the name to nearby Collier Street at Baxenden and was probably one of George Hargreaves' concerns. The most likely site is in the disturbed ground in the allotment on the left of the lane that is a continuation of Parker Street.

CHAPELS COAL PIT   SD695235

This could have been one of 3 shafts marked coal pit, old coal pit, or bottoms coal pit on the 1848 OS map in the Goosehouse area of Blackburn.

Darwen Advertiser, February 6th 1985:- Blackburn Council's Engineering Department is capping 3 coal shafts in the Goosehouse area. Mr Alan Peake, Chief Engineer, said they knew of the existence of the shafts from old mining plans, and it seemed prudent to cap them. Landscaping is taking place in connection with the development of land at Goosehouse for industry. Mr Peake said 2 are at Goosehouse and the third behind Vicarage Terrace. The soil and clay is removed from the top and then a concrete raft put on the solid rock before the soil is put back. The capping is to NCB specifications and no structures are allowed within 10 metres of the shafts, said Mr Peake. The shafts were part of the Chapels coal pit, shown on the 1847 map. They could have been used by personnel or as air shafts.

CLAYTON - OLD ENGINE   SD753328
- NEW ENGINE   SD747324

This was the name given to two distinct areas of mining marked on the 1844 OS Map to the NE and the SW of Hyndburn Bridge, between Clayton-le-Moors and Great Harwood. The first, at the bottom of Mill Lane and across the bridge over the River Hyndburn, consisted of a coal pit and old engine, suggesting winding or pumping arrangements. The second was in Duxbury Wood, on the left past the Hyndburn Bridge public house (formerly the Dog and Partridge), but before the turn-off to Great Harwood. Here were two coal pits, a weighing machine and a new engine, suggesting later workings than the old engine.

The Clayton Collieries were worked by the Lomax family of nearby Clayton Hall, and date from the late 18th and early 19th centuries. Shallow shafts were sunk to the Arley Mine (depth unknown) and the workings were extensive enough to justify the expense of installing engines. These pits were abandoned around 1855 and are not mentioned in the *List of Mines* for 1869. The site of the old engine is reached by going down Mill Lane to a bridge over Hyndburn Brook, then turning right into the field, roughly midway between 2 iron pipes across the river. Agriculture has reclaimed the site, but coal mined at Clayton Colliery nearly 150 years ago can still be picked up off the path. Another path and footbridge over Hyndburn Brook, behind the Hyndburn Bridge public house, goes past the site of the new engine pits. There is little evidence of coal mining today, though a house on the left of this path is reputed to have been the beam engine house for the new engine at the collieries.

Children, including one 7 year old, were employed at these mines during the 1840s, when 57 men were also employed. Ventilation was by means of a fire at one of the shafts.

Blackburn Times, June 7th 1856:- *On Saturday last, Edward Whitaker, aged 24 years and of Great Harwood, met with a violent death whilst working at the shaft bottom in one of Mr Lomax's mines. A large coal slipped out of the basket that was being wound up, and fell upon his head with great force, inflicting such injuries that death resulted within a few hours. The occurrence was quite accidental.*

CLOSE NOOK RISHTON
Nothing remains of this pit which was located north of Rishton, near Close Nook Farm and beyond the dismantled railway. It was worked by the Dunkenhalgh Colliery Company in 1879.

CLOSES   SD710228
A number of small pits, off the Roman Road and above Higher Waterside, were worked during the early 1840s. At the top of Harwood's Lane, in Hoddlesden, a track leads down towards Waterside Works. At the first gate, a footpath on the left passes a water-filled sandstone quarry and Closes Colliery is marked by an area of disturbed ground a few yards further on. From here the ruined Closes Farm from which the colliery took its name can be seen. A number of other shafts were sunk over to the right. The pit is marked on the 1848 OS Map, and had an engine house, reservoir and boiler, suggesting steam power was used for raising the coals.

COB WALL PIT   SD695290
This is probably the old colliery marked on the 1844 OS Map. The shaft was 80 yards to a 24 inch thick coal, possibly the Upper Mountain Seam. The site was roughly at the corner of the Northrop works, off Phillips Road, Blackburn. Nothing else is known.

CONEY   SD683214
William Pierce opened these drift working into the Dogshaw Seam in the late 1840s or early 1850s. According to the *Collieries of Lancashire*, however, by 1879 the Coney Coal and Fireclay Co. Ltd was working the pit for fireclay, along with the Lower Yard Seam. Offices and other buildings were located at Wood Street, Darwen, where a tramway ran up to the drift entrance. John Taylor, a paper maker, may also have had an interest in this colliery, which was abandoned in 1881.

COPY CLOUGH   SD742293
The site is best approached via Church Hall and Peel Bank towards the canal. Cross the swing bridge and go down the middle lane. Copy Clough Colliery is then on the left. A triangular concrete marker indicates the position of the shaft, while the rubble close by was the engine house.

The shaft, sunk by Haworth, Barnes and Co. around 1838, was 228 feet deep to the Lower Mountain Mine. Coal winding stopped in 1873, though the pit was retained for ventilating Enfield Pit and Dunkenhalgh Colliery.

A ginney track took the output to a canal wharf. An inventory by Peter Wright Pickup lists the following at the surface:- two vertical high pressure steam engines, with 30 inch stroke cylinders and 9 inch bore, valued at £150; circular steam boilers, 28 foot by 8 foot, with two flues, 18 Galloway tubes etc, valued at £300; wooden roof and cupola over pit top, valued at £9 16s 6d; and 24 tubs at 10s 0d each. Equipment in buildings on the surface, including a private office, counting house, weighing machine house, store room, yard, back store room, wheelwrights' shop, oil store, tub shop, mechanic's shop, smithy and stable (with 3 horses named Tom, Jack and Fanny) was valued at £260. At the pit bottom were: two vertical engines, with 16 inch stroke cylinders, worth £100; gears and shafting worth £50; a ventilation furnace worth £5 10s 0d; 1350 yards of signal wire and pulleys worth £5 12s 6d; and the steam engine in the middle of Jig Brow, which had two vertical 20 inch stroke and 10 inch bore cylinders worth £130 0s 0d.[5]

COUPE   SD774265
Thought to have been one of George Hargreaves' collieries, dating from around the 1820s, this was probably a drift mine. It was abandoned by the mid 1840s with the development of the Baxenden Collieries, but was on land now used as a car park behind Baxenden Conservative Club on Manchester Road.

CRANBERRY MOSS   SD706206
These pits were worked between Bolton Road, at Darwen, and Blacksnape village. James Briggs, a coal master, may have worked them in the 1830s. James Barlow was working the pit in 1869, and Ralph Entwistle and Co. Ltd, of Darwen, worked it during 1879. In the 1890s, Richard Walkden was manager with 50 men underground and 6 on the surface. The Mountian and the Half Yard seams were worked and fireclay was mined. A number of shafts were sunk in this area, but the main winding shaft appears to have been at Darwen Fireclay Works on Cranberry Lane, Darwen. These works were started by Ralph Entwistle around 1860, mainly to work fireclay, though coal was mined too. Products manufactured included chimney pots, pipes and firebricks. Several shafts were sunk near the Sough Railway Tunnel. In 1890, a steam-driven winding-engine, by Turner, Bury Brothers of Darwen, was installed at a new shaft here. The company went into voluntary liquidation in 1914, and the pits were abandoned the following year.

Blackburn Times, May 17th 1884:- *Mr J. Robinson, coroner, held an inquest on Wednesday on Thomas Walkden, 12, drawer, who died on Tuesday. He was the son of Thomas Walkden, collier, of 16 Rosehill Street, and worked with him at Messrs Entwistle and Co's. coal pit at Cranberry Lane. When going up the jig brow on Tuesday, he was jammed against a post by a wagon that had broken loose from the chain and fatally injured. The jury returned a verdict of Accidental Death, leaving the question of liability open.*

Blackburn Times, May 22nd 1909:- *On Monday an inquest was held by Mr D.N. Haslewood, deputy coroner, at the Bolton Road newsrooms, Darwen, on Richard Harwood, 44, collier, of 18 Willie Street, Sough, Darwen, who was killed at Messrs Entwistle and Co's Cranberry Lane Colliery last Friday. Mr Cooper (Hindle and Son) and Mr A.F. Greenhalgh, of Bolton represented the firm. Mr J. Gerrard, Inspector of Mines, and George Nicholson, of the Lancashire and Cheshire Miners' Federation, were also present. Michael Harwood, weaver, 18 Willie Street, Darwen, said that the deceased was his brother, and was employed at Cranberry Lane Pipe Works. He was not married. John Burns, 1 Rockery Cottages, said that on Friday he was working with Harwood. While he was in the act of falling some earth, Harwood came to his place. Burns told him to stand back, but, before Harwood had time, some 3 or 4 cwts of earth fell on him and crashed him onto a wagon. Burns got assistance to remove the earth, and they found Harwood was dead. Harwood had no business being in Burns' place. Mr Gerrard said he did not blame Burns for what happened and added that this was the second fatality to occur at this pit recently. PC Little said Harwood's face was badly damaged, and there was a wound at the back of the head. A verdict of Accidental Death was returned.*

DANDY ROW COLLIERY   SD701231

The site of this colliery, listed in the *Catalogue of Abandoned Mines,* is not known, but it must have been in the Eccleshill area of Darwen as Joseph Place's Eccleshills Colliery broke into the old workings. There is a Dandy Row on the Roman Road, near Pot House Lane, Darwen.

DEWHURST   SD772262

This drift had 2 entrances to the south-west, on the hill above Railway Pit, Baxenden. The travelling road was 3 foot by 4 foot, turning south-east, and the haulage road was 9 foot by 7 foot. Both drifts were stone lined. The pit worked with Railway Pit, using pillar and stall to exploit the Upper Mountain Mine, which averaged 1 foot 6 inches in height. The drift was possibly named after the main man who drove it, a common practice in this area. An air pit, or shaft, in Tom Dule Clough, was connected with the Dewhurst Drift. The pit was abandoned by 1902.

Accrington Times, September 5th 1874:- *Mr Hargreaves, coroner, held an inquest on Wednesday at the Great Eastern Hotel, on Joseph Bordley, 23, of Dowry Street. Mr Dickinson, Inspector of Mines, Mr Bolton, agent, and Mr Hudson, manager to Messrs George Hargreaves, were present. Rebecca Bordley, mother of the deceased, said that a fortnight last Monday he came home, sat on the sofa and began to cry. He said he had been hurt on the forehead and right side, but would not tell her how it had happened. He was in a good deal of pain and went to bed. He vomited and had diarrhoea, then had nothing to eat afterwards up to the time of his death on Sunday night. Mrs Bordley told Mr Bolton that Mr Hudson came to see her son when he was in bed, but he would tell them nothing. John Leonard Clarkson,*

10, said he was taking a full tub to the shaft in Dewhurst's Drift, and he was without light. He met Joseph Bordley, who had 2 tubs with him and wanted help. Clarkson gave his tub a push and went to help Bordley, but his full tub dashed against an empty one which Bordley was pushing with his head and hurt him. Mr Hudson produced a plan of the workings, and explained that Bordley was drawing water from one part of the mine and tipping it into another. Having taken the water, he should have returned by the empty road, which was about 12 yards further. To save this, he went along the full road, and thus came into collision. Thomas Stanton, drawer, said he was about 10 yards from Bordley when he ran against the full tub, which was stationary. Bordley always went along the full road and he usually called out, but did not do so this time. Stanton added that the accident took place before breakfast time, and that Bordley worked until 2 o'clock. Evidence was then given on the laying out of the body, which had a bruise on the forehead extending to the nose, and a mark on the right side. The jury thought Bordley was to blame for the matter, and returned a verdict of Accidental Death.

DILL HALL   SD746299

Joseph Barnes sank Dill Hall Pit in the mid 1850s and its shaft had a wooden headgear, with two 5-foot-diameter pulleys. Coal was transported by a tramway down past Dill Hall to the shaft at Enfield Colliery. Two egg-ended boilers provided steam to the 2 diagonal steam engines with 5 foot stroke cylinders and a 10 inch bore, valued at £460.[3] Coal was raised here till around 1860, when this particular pit became a ventilation shaft, and Enfield Pit became the coal winding shaft. There are no remains of this shaft, as the site has been built on.

The Dunkenhalgh Colliery Co. worked Dill Hall in 1879, according to a colliery index. The company was formed in 1876 by the Exors of John Hargreaves, the Burnley colliery owners; Thomas Brooks of Towneley Collieries, Burnley; and Peter Wright Pickup of Rishton Colliery, to run the Church collieries. According to the Geological Survey, the shaft was 384 feet deep to the Lower Mountain Mine. It was near the junction of the present day Queen's Road West, and immediately in front of Dill Hall Farm.

Accrington Free Press, July 18th 1859:- A collier called Rishton, 34 and of Church, was working with a youth in Mr Barnes's coal-pit, when a firedamp arose and burnt him so severely that he died on Tuesday night, but the youth miraculously escaped. The inquest will be held on Rishton today.

Burnley Advertiser, July 1859:- William Rushton was summoned by Mr Joseph Barnes of Church for breach of the colliery rules at Church. The underlooker, on behalf of Mr Barnes, said that last Friday he was at the pit bottom when he saw Rushton at work with the top off his lamp. As several serious accidents have taken place from similar offences, Mr Barnes was determined to bring all such cases before the magistrates. Rushton was severely reprimanded, and the Bench told the underlooker that they would deal with the next case with the full vigour of the law.

In spite of Mr Barnes' determination to eliminate explosions, 4 men were killed just 6 years later at Dill Hall Pit.

Burnley Express, April 15th 1865:- On Tuesday, 4 men were suffocated at Dill Hall coal-pit, Church. They were John Cecil, 23, married; John Illingworth, 18, drawer; George Eastham, 17, drawer; and John Duckworth, 14. Cecil was a hooker-on, and about 16.15, the 3 drawers brought their tubs to him. About the same time some colliers nearby felt a strong rush of afterdamp and, supposing an explosion had taken place, went to the spot, where they discovered the bodies. A portion of the roof had been dislodged, yet there was no sign of fire on the bodies or on the few clothes they wore. The men used locked safety lamps, but Cecil had an exposed light, as he worked in fresh air. None of the pitmen reported an explosion of firedamp having taken place. The bodies were removed to an adjoining public house to await the coroner's inquiry.

John Cecil's working with a naked flame indicates that this shaft was downcast as far as ventilation was concerned, but, in spite of further research, no more information on this incident has been found. The probable cause of death was afterdamp, a suffocating gas left after a firedamp explosion.

DOGSHAW   SD868201

There were several drift workings in the Dogshaw area of Darwen. Mr Walsh operated one pit during the early 1830s, while Messrs Hilton of Old Darwen Paper Mills, leased the mining rights around 1840. Eccles Shorrock drove a new drift mine circa 1850 to intercept the Lower Mountain Mine below Duckshaw Farm. Eccles Shorrock and Co. also built India Mill between 1859 and 1870, but the cost of the building, along with the Cotton Famine, ruined Shorrock. However, he rose again, with Richard Eccles of Lower Darwen Mills and others, as a promoter of the India Mills Cotton Spinning Company, formed in 1874. A mineral line at Dogshaw Colliery crossed the goit that provided water for the Darwen Paper Mill and carried coal from the colliery to the India and Darwen Mills. At one time the pit employed over 50 men. The *List of Mines* for 1869 records it being worked by Eccles Shorrock, Brother and Co., but it was abandoned shortly afterwards.

Blackburn Standard, March 20th 1850:- At Darwen Petty Sessions last Friday, Thomas Isherwood charged John Mather for violently assaulting him on Tuesday week at the bottom of a coal pit. Isherwood said Mather was on a basket at the time and kicked and hit him on the face several times. Isherwood thought the blows had deprived him of the sight of an eye, and he was so much hurt that he had not been able to work since. Mr S.H. Waith, surgeon, said he had seen Isherwood on Tuesday week, and that his eye was cut down to the bone. Isherwood ought not to have left his home, as he was not yet fit for work. The magistrates fined Mather 10s and costs, in default to be committed to gaol for 14 days. They also ordered him to find securities to keep the peace, in default to be committed to gaol for a month.

Blackburn Standard, March 5th 1851:- *For several days the men in Dogshaw Colliery, Darwen, were inconvenienced by smoke finding its way into the workings without any apparent cause. This continued up to Monday week, when a search was made and, in the remote part of some old workings, a complete apparatus for illicit distillation was discovered. The still had been erected close to one of the pillars which had ignited from the fire in use in the furnace, and this had spread to other parts adjacent, causing the smoke which led to the search. Information was forwarded to the police and PS Fearan and PC Shaw, together with the underlooker, his son, and Mr Henry Shorrock, went to the spot. The old workings were entered by a drift, about 40 yards long, near the end of which a recess had been made. In this were 4 short bars, of one inch red iron, one of which was heavily loaded at one end, and a collier's pick, evidently put there to be used in case of attack. After waiting to see if anyone came, they struggled to remove the still, but found it impossible to remove the other apparatus without knocking it to pieces. Strong suspicion fell on a party who had been convicted of a similar offence, and who had been seen in the neighbourhood twice that day before the discovery was made.*

Manchester Guardian, October 16th 1850:- *On Friday last the young man who had care of the wagons that convey coals from Darwen Moor to Darwen Mills, met with a serious accident. John Holden, who was in charge of the full wagons which are calculated to hold 2 tons of coal each and are hauled down an incline of rails by a rope, was applying the brake when the 2 leading wagons ran off the rails. The end of the brake, an iron bar 3 inches in circumference, was driven through the thick part of his thigh. Medical assistance was given by Mr Clarke, surgeon, and he is progressing well.*

Blackburn Times, June 18th 1859:- *On Wednesday morning near Dogshaw Colliery there was considerable activity and rejoicing at the starting of the first locomotive engine to run on part of the colliery tramway. The engine, which is entirely new, was constructed at Darwen Mills under the supervision of Mr John Hodkinson. It is about 12 HP and was completed and placed on the lines on Tuesday. The next morning the roar of cannon announced the event, and a number of flags were flying. There assembled were Mr and Mrs R. Ashton, Miss Ashton, Miss Shorrock, and Mr Shorrock etc. A part of the tender was cushioned for the ladies and gentlemen, and, when they had taken their seats, away flew 'Pluto' — for that is the name given to the engine — in fine style amid the waving of banners, the reverberations of the artillery, and cheers of the men. In the evening a number of the men sat down to supper at the Bowling Green Inn.*

DUCKWORTH HALL   SD725267

This colliery is reached by taking the footpath to the left of the Duckworth Hall public house, then turning right after a short distance. The site is marked by two capped shafts, with triangular markers, in the fields on either side of this muddy lane. The mine had a steam pumping engine in the 1830s and George Yates leased it to Simpson and Young in the early 1850s. The shafts were then deepened to the Lower Mountain Mine, and eventually the workings connected with those of Aspen Colliery. The pit closed in 1884, but is described as a Pumping Pit, possibly for the Aspen Colliery, in the *List of Mines* for 1896.

Blackburn Mail, November 1st 1826:- *Mr J. Hargreaves held an inquest at Oswaldtwistle on the 9th ult. on George Taylor, who worked in a coal mine there. On the 5th ult. he was at work when a large stone separated from the roof and landed on his head, fracturing his skull. After lingering in great agony, he died on the 7th ult. A verdict of Accidental Death was recorded.*

Blackburn Times, October 17th 1857:- *On Thursday week an explosion of firedamp took place at Messrs Simpson and Young's No. 2 pit, Duckworth Hall, Oswaldtwistle, killing Robert East, 16, and John Woodhead, 10, drawer, who lived with his father at Oswaldtwistle. John Whewell and his son, of Guide, and John Duckworth, of Shadsworth, were very much burnt. On Monday John Hargreaves, coroner, held an inquest. Joseph Dickinson, Inspector of Mines, assisted in the investigation. John Duckworth said Robert East had been working for him for about 4 years, coming from Blackburn Workhouse when he was about 12 years old. He added that East had no relations except a half brother in Blackburn and a brother who was a soldier. John Woodhead was also a drawer, working for John Whewell. About 7.00 a.m. on Thursday week, Duckworth went down the pit with East and Woodhead, Thomas Gorton, and 2 other boys. When they arrived at the bottom, he and East set out together to go to the place where they usually stopped. John Whewell and his two drawers (his son and Woodhead), were with them. At Whewell's request, East went for some candles. He took his tub and a naked, lighted candle. Almost immediately East had gone, Duckworth heard a loud crack, and saw blaze coming along the roof. He lay down to save himself, then rose and called out to East. He came and they went towards the shaft until they came to some tubs which they got into and were wheeled back to the shaft. East was very much burnt, and the skin seemed to be ploughed on his arms and legs. Duckworth, who was burnt on his right side, went with him to the top of the pit, and they went home together. Mr Howarth, surgeon, attended them at home, but East died that night. Duckworth said that Woodhead was very much burnt and had been near him when the explosion took place. He also said that it was usual in this pit for the workpeople to get about with lighted candles, using them without covers. He was not aware of any firedamp in the pit before Thursday and on the previous Tuesday he had sent East to inform Mr Holden, the underlooker, that his candle burnt clear, as Holden did not visit the works every day. On the Monday morning, before the explosion, Duckworth had pointed out a seam or crack above his head to Holden, who told him to be cautious. The light of his candle was affected and Holden thought it was as result of sulphur coming from the seam. Holden told Duckworth to let him know if the sulphur became stronger. George Howarth, manager of Messrs Simpson and Young's coal works, said he had worked at collieries for 8 years and the pit in question had been at work for 3 years. He had not been aware of any firedamp before the explosion. On Friday he went down with Mr Dickinson, the inspector, to view the place where the explosion happened and saw the seam in the roof, through which he thought the firedamp had made its way. The place where John Duckworth and John Woodhead were working was at the far end of the heading. The seam was also there, but the spot where the explosion took place was about 20 yards from the end. The ventilation there was imperfect. There was an underworking going on. If that had been completed, this accident might not have happened. Howarth thought that, if Holden was aware of the presence of firedamp on Monday and said so to Duckworth, he had done all he could be expected to do. He did not blame Holden, but thought he should have examined the pit before the workpeople went into it. He was provided with a safety lamp and had a copy of the rules for the government of this pit. Joseph Woodhead, of New Lane, Oswaldtwistle, labourer, said that John Woodhead was his son and was 10 years old. He was very much burnt when he was taken home about 9 o'clock on Thursday morning. Mr Howarth, surgeon, came to see him, but he died on Saturday morning after suffering a great deal of pain. William Holden, of Oswaldtwistle, after a caution, said he had been the underlooker for Mr Simpson at Duckworth Hall Colliery for 4 years, and had never seen the appearance of gas to any dangerous extent. He corroborated Duckworth's evidence about the seam and the sulphur on the Monday and Tuesday, and added that on Wednesday there was no work going on. He had not completed the ventilation of that part when the explosion happened, because no danger was apprehended and, as the firedamp appeared so trifling on Monday, he did not think it necessary to stop the workings. He did not inform the manager of the presence of sulphur on Monday as he did not think it was dangerous and he did not send down any person on the Tuesday and Thursday to examine the pit, because he thought the danger had passed. Six or eight months before they saw a little firedamp, but did not report that to the manager. Mr Dickinson said that the first general rule requires the proprietors of the pit to provide proper ventilation. As firedamp had been found in this place on the Monday preceding the accident, the underlooker was bound by the 42nd special rule to report it to the manager, in order that proper precautions might be taken. Mr Dickinson found nothing wrong with the general ventilation of the pit, but the part where the explosion took place was stagnant as it was too far in advance. The underlooker ought to have reported the previous appearance of sulphur, and a fireman ought to have been appointed. The coroner then read over the evidence, pointing out to the jury each particular part which showed neglect by William Holden. The jury then reached a unanimous verdict of*

Manslaughter against William Holden, and recommended that Messrs Simpson and Young in future use Davy lamps in the pit. William Holden was committed to Kirkdale jail for trial at the next Liverpool assizes.

James Whewell, the son of John, died of his burns on the same date. He was 9 years old and working undergound 15 years after the Coal Mines Act of 1842. This example, and a number of others, show that the law was flouted flagrantly in this area and yet no prosecutions were brought.

DUCKWORTH HILL SD729264
Not to be confused with Duckworth Hall Colliery, this refers to two shafts on Duckworth Hill which were recorded by the Geological Survey. It is mentoned in the *Report on Child Labour in Coal-Mines 1841*:-

Duckworth Hill Colliery, George Yates, proprietor. In the township of Oswaldtwistle, parish of Whalley. Girls are employed here as well as boys. The number and ages of male children are:- 3 of 11 years, and 8 of 12 years. Of the female children, the number and ages are:- 1 of 10 years, 1 of 11 years and 2 of 12 years. The hours of work are 9, the wages average 5 shillings per week. Young persons employed at the colliery:- 3 of 13 years, 4 of 14 years, 5 of 15 years, 4 of 16 years, 6 of 17 years. The females are:- 2 of 13, 1 of 14, and 1 of 15. All the above are paid by day wages. There are 31 adults employed in this mine. Horses and asses are employed to draw up the coal. All those listed above are drawers, and draw by the belt and chain. The length of the runs are 120 yards, the weight of the coal drawn is one and a half cwt. The seam here is very thin, being only 18 inches high. The adults, therefore, cannot be employed as drawers. The pit is 28 yards deep. No particular system of ventilation is adopted.

DUNKENHALGH (PARK) SD739295
This was a large colliery, employing some 300 men at its peak. According to the Geological Survey, the shaft was 171 feet deep and was sunk in 1837. The pit was wet and gassy, which is an unusual combination, and in its early days used a 35 foot diameter, by 7 foot wide, waterwheel for coal winding. The wheel, along with its iron buckets and associated gearing etc., was valued at £550 0s 0d.

Until 1872, Messrs Howarth, Barnes and Boardman leased the colliery from Mr Petre. He then worked the pit until 1874 when the Dunkenhalgh Colliery Co. got a 40 year lease, at a yearly rental of £3,000 plus royalties, and invested £10,000 in labour and equipment to start working the pit. By 1884, however, the company was in severe financial difficulties and tried to re-negotiate the lease. A prolonged legal dispute began after some shady dealing by Peter Wright Pickup (Peter Pickup's son) and the firm's directors. This led to the abandonment of the pit.

Blackburn Standard, March 17th 1841:- *On Saturday last an inquest was held at the Thorn public-house, Church, on John Eastwood and Evan Whittaker. Both boys were 12 and were drawers in Messrs Howarth, Barnes and Boardman's coal-pit in Dunkenhalgh Park. Last Thursday night at about 10.15, the banksman was letting them down the pit in a tub, but when they had only descended a yard or two, the ropes broke. They fell to the bottom, a distance of 75 yards, and were killed on the spot. The pit, which is a new one, is much affected by foul air and, to purify it, a fire has been kept at the bottom for a day or two. The rope, which was also new, had coiled at the bottom the last time it was used. It had been let down and had caught fire. One of the men who was going down into the pit by the other end of the rope met the burning rope coming up, and shouted at once to the banksman to tell him of it, but owing to the noise made by water falling down the sides of the mine he could not make him understand what he said. A verdict of Accidental Death was recorded.*

Blackburn Standard, September 22nd 1841:- *An inquest was held last Thursday at the Thorn public house, Church, on Edward Spencer, 20, miner at Messrs Haworth, Barnes and Boardman's coal mine in Dunkenhalgh Park. The mine is subject to firedamp and there have been several explosions recently, but no fatalities. On Monday morning the overlooker went through the workings with a safety lamp, and there appeared to be no danger. At that time Spencer was at work in his proper place. But, shortly after the overlooker had gone, Spencer told a fellow workman that he was going to steal a pillar, and to do so went into a part of the mine that is not inspected, where he had no business to go. Immediately he got there an explosion took place from the candle which he held in his hand. He was much burnt*

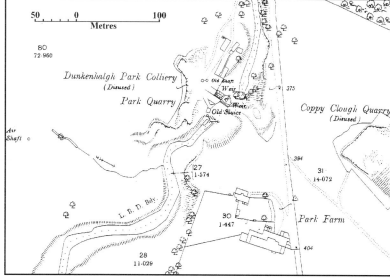

Fig. 6.

45

about the face and body and died on the evening of the next day. There are about 26 persons employed in the mine, under penalty not to leave the place they are set to work. A verdict of Accidental Death was recorded.

Burnley Express, August 10th 1872:- *The adjourned inquest on Geoffrey Lomax 45, William Walsh, 35, and Thomas Johnson, 30, who died from the effects of the colliery explosion at Dunkenhalgh Pit, Church, was resumed yesterday before Mr Hargreaves, coroner. Mr Dickinson, Inspector of Mines, was present. Richard Taylor, miner, stated that colliers could light their lamps through a safety-lamp without opening it, and he showed the jury how it was done. He thought if William Parkinson* [who was injured in the explosion] *opened his lamp, it would be to snuff it, or to have more light. Robert Wilson, miner, said there was gas close to a throw (fault) where Parkinson worked. Lomax had told them to be cautious. William Sharples, underlooker, said he found Parkinson's lamp bottom in his place after the explosion, and on Thursday Parkinson told him where to find the top. The lamp was produced and was perfect and locked properly. Richard Morley, fireman, said gas escaped from a seam seven and a half yards from where Parkinson worked. It was bratticed off with cloth four and a half yards from where he worked. He visited the place at 6.30 and 9.30 on the day of the explosion, and found it safe to work in. The ventilation was good. He could not account for the explosion, except by supposing Parkinson had gone out of his place. All the other lamps were locked. Richard Taylor, one of the injured men, said he saw Parkinson with his lamp top off 3 times on the day of the explosion. He found Parkinson asleep a short time before the explosion. He must have opened his lamp after he saw him. Summing up, the coroner pointed out that Parkinson was legally responsible for the explosion. He directed the jury to return a verdict of Manslaughter against Parkinson and they did so.*

Accrington Times, August 17th 1872:- *The jury which last week examined the deaths of Geoffrey Lomax, William Walsh and Thomas Johnson returned a verdict of Manslaughter against William Parkinson of Church Kirk, one of the injured men. At the time he was in a critical condition, and the knowledge of the verdict seems to have made him worse. After it was given, he refused to take any nourishment and wished to die. His death took place at 6.30 on Monday morning. Mr Hargreaves, coroner, held an inquest on Tuesday at Church Kirk. Parkinson's widow confirmed that he was 42 and had been burned on the face and arms in an explosion at Dunkenhalgh pit on Thursday week. The jury, by direction of the coroner, returned a verdict that he died from Misadventure. From inquiries made yesterday, it appears that Lomax and Taylor are soon likely to recover from their injuries. Berry is the most burnt of the survivors and hopes are entertained that he may recover.*

Accrington Times, August 9th 1873:- *Mr Petre of Dunkenhalgh, owner of the Church and Rishton Collieries, has generously arranged to give the men in his employ a trip to Blackpool. Upwards of 400 are estimated to go on the train.*

Accrington Times, June 19th 1875:- *At the County Petty Sessions, Blackburn, on Wednesday, before Col. Bowden, J. Johnston, J. Briggs, J. Fish and W. Birtwistle Esq., 26 colliers in the employ of the Dunkenhalgh Colliery Company were summoned for leaving their work without notice. The defendants wanted a play day and consequently did not attend work on Monday morning, May 31st. The amount of damages claimed was 5 shillings per man. Mr Baldwin of Burnley appeared on behalf of the Company, and Mr Radcliffe for the defendants. All the cases were settled except two, in which the defendants paid 1 shilling each as compensation.*

By 1881 the Dunkenhalgh Colliery Company was also having problems with Mr Petre, the colliery's owner, over the renewal of the lease, as they felt the terms were too onerous to allow a profit to be made. In February of that year, the dead rent was reduced from £3000 to £2000 a year, but, as the following report shows, the problems continued.

Blackburn Standard, May 5th 1883:- *The Dunkenhalgh Collieries, Rishton, have for a period of about 9 years been worked under a lease by a company, Mr Petre of Rishton being the owner. On May 1st the lease expired and the company, having some grievance, failed to make terms with Mr Petre and either resolved or were compelled to give up the pits altogether. About 100 men and boys were thrown out of work, and men were hired from Burnley to clear all the working materials away. A large waterwheel, which had been in the engine house for about 20 years and was the principal wheel for pumping water out of the 3 pits, was broken up and thrown down one of the shafts. The engine house was pulled down, the conducting rods broken and all the gearing connected with the pumping machinery destroyed. As a result, all the pits are rapidly filling with water, and it is roughly estimated that to set them in working order again several thousands pounds will have to be expended.*

According to the *Catalogue of Plans of Abandoned Mines*, Dunkenhalgh Colliery was abandoned in 1884, so it seems that no-one gained any benefit from the prolonged and perplexing court case – reported in full in the *Accrington Times* for April 4th 1885 – brought by the Dunkenhalgh Colliery Co. against Peter Wright Pickup, its former manager and secretary, who seems to have been trying to negotiate a lease for himself from Mr Petre at the same time as he was supposed to be negotiating one for the company. They were trying to claim damages against him for improper conduct, but Vice Chancellor Bristowe, who heard the case at the Manchester sittings of the Chancery Court of Lancashire, was of the opinion that a sufficient case had not been made out and the case was dismissed.

DUNNYSHOP PITS   SD745276

In the early 19th century, several deep shafts were sunk in the Dunnyshop area of Accrington, possibly by George Hargreaves & Co. Reputed to have been linked with the drift at Woodnook, they were back-filled by the late 1890s and, except for the name Coal Pit Lane, nothing remains.

ECCLESHILL   SD692235

This colliery is mentioned in *The Collieries of Lancashire in 1879*, when it was being worked by James Hacking.

Blackburn Standard, June 1851:- *In an incident at a drift mine near Davy Field Eccleshill (Darwen) a number of miners became trapped by a roof fall. Several people from the neighbourhood were soon on the scene, and working from 11 in the morning till 10 at night they finally freed the men. One of the miners is reported to have cut 4 shillings worth of coal to augment his wages while all this was going on!*

The *Catalogue of Abandoned Mines* lists a colliery named Eccleshill, along with workings at Tithe Barn, as being abandoned in 1882. It also notes that Eccleshill Colliery and Fireclay Works broke into the workings of Dandy Row, Flash and Princess Collieries.

ECCLESHILL COLLIERY AND FIRECLAY WORKS SD692235

This pit, sunk by Joseph Place and Sons of Hoddlesden Collieries, reached the Lower Mountain Mine at a depth of 276 feet in 1892. A pipe works, near the pit head on Goosehouse Lane, was built by the mid 1890s. The pit was abandoned through exhaustion in 1916, when the *List of Mines* recorded 32 underground and 2 surface workers, but Hoddlesden Collieries continued to supply raw materials to the pipe works. The latter closed in the late 1940s after a serious fire. The site is now a car wreckers' yard on Goosehouse Lane, above Darwen roadstone quarry. The chimney at Eccleshill Works was felled in August 1957. The 2 brick pumphouses, which stand over the old shafts, were built by Darwen Corporation in the 1950s.

Darwen News, July 23rd 1892:- *The new pit shaft, sunk by Messrs Joseph Place and Sons at Eccleshill, has proved successful, with coal being found on Monday morning. Messrs J. Place and Sons are the only colliery proprietors in Darwen who work pits on an extensive scale, and sell part of their production. The Hoddlesden Collieries were taken by Messrs John and Joseph Place about 50 years ago. For close upon 30 years they were worked by Mr Joseph Place and, since his death, by his sons, Messrs J.E. and W.H. Place. There are 2 mines at Hoddlesden, one known as the 18 Inch Mine, and the other the Yard Mine, but the average thickness of coal is between 2 and 3 feet. When the Hoddlesden Branch Line was built by the Lancashire and Yorkshire Railway Company, Messrs Place decided, instead of getting a quantity of shale from the top of the roof in order to work the thin seam, to get fireclay, which was several feet thick, and use it for making fire bricks and sanitary ware. Having the railway for transport made this a very profitable part of the business and they have developed one of the largest sanitary pipe works in the Kingdom. Messrs Place and Sons are now employing about 300 hands at Hoddlesden. About 15 months ago the firm leased the coal under the land belonging to the executors of Messrs Hodgson's trustees, and started to sink a shaft 13 feet in diameter, but they*

PLATE IV Eccleshill Colliery and Pipeworks (By permisson of Ann Stokes).

soon met a considerable quantity of water, and pumps were ordered from Messrs Haythorn, Davey of Leeds. Each pump gave a 16 inch lift, allowing the water problem to be overcome. The shaft has been sunk 92 yards and has been bricked round to the bottom, with the exception of about 30 feet which will be completed in about a month's time. Three shifts of 6 men have worked 24 hours a day to sink the shaft. The coal reached is 19 inches thick and, with 6 inches of cannel, is 25 inches all told. Under this, it is hoped to come to 6 feet of fireclay, which is as important to Messrs Place as the coal, as they intend to carry on at their Eccleshill works exactly the same kind of business as is being carried on so successfully at Hoddlesden. When the works are in full swing, there will be employment for at least 200 men. By an Act of Parliament, no pit in which more than 25 men are employed below ground can be worked without 2 shafts, and the second shaft has already been sunk to a depth of 40 yards. As it is unlikely that the water difficulty will impede progress, the shaft will be completed in 3 or 4 months' time. The work has been successfully carried on at the new pit by Mr W. Taylor, the manager, who was formerly the manager at Whitebirk Collieries. The Eccleshill estate will, if the pits are fully employed, last over 30 or 40 years, and the additional leases which Messrs Place have taken out at their Hoddlesden Coalfield will last for even longer. The Eccleshill Colliery has been provided with a 35 yard iron chimney, standing on massive foundations 5 feet high.

PLATE V
Joseph Place (1809-1881)
(By permisson of Ann Stokes).

Darwen News, December 5th 1908:- *George Marsden, 25, collier, of School Lane, Guide, was killed on Saturday at Messrs Joseph Place and Sons Ltd's Eccleshill Colliery, when he was struck upon the head by a rock fall. He received terrible injuries and died almost instantaneously. Mr H.J. Robinson, District Coroner, held an inquest at Darwen police station on Tuesday. Mr F. Hindle (Messrs. Hindle and Son) attended on behalf of the employers. Mr Gerrard, Inspector of Mines, was present, as was Mr John McGurk, agent for the Lancashire and Cheshire Miners' Federation. Mary Marsden, widow of the deceased, said he left his home shortly before 6.00 a.m. on Saturday to go to work. William Thomas Tomlinson, of Higher Snape Street, Darwen, drawer, said he was working with Marsden, getting clay from the pit. He last saw Marsden at 9.15. He told Mr Hindle that there were 3 props when he last saw Marsden alive. James Edward Hartley, miner, of Snape Street, Darwen, said he was working 20 yards away from Marsden on the morning of the accident, which occurred about 9.45. He did not hear anything, but his attention was called by James Mather, a drawer. The roof fall had covered Marsden and, when Hartley removed the earth, he found him in a sitting position with his head crushed between his legs. It took about 90 seconds to get him out and he was then quite dead. The fall was a big stone, which dropped in a solid mass and broke up into smaller pieces. It would be about 5 feet long, 4 feet wide and about 19 inches thick at the broad end. There had been props under the stone and it seemed that Marsden was about to erect a prop when the accident happened. Hartley told Mr Hindle that there was a good supply of props and it was the duty of the miner to erect their own props. The Coroner said that Marsden seemed to have been doing his work in the usual manner when a large stone came upon him, and he had no chance to get out of the way. The jury returned a verdict of Accidental Death.* See also: *Evening Telegraph*, August 7th 1957

EDMUND   **SD780273**

This early pit, marked on a redrawn map of 1784 in Accrington Reference Library, was near Meadow Top Farm, beyond Baxenden Golf Course. No trace of it remains, other than a tramway embankment, branching from the main tramway embankment and running east to west to form the northern boundary of the golf course. Along with George Pit lower down, Edmund Pit worked the Lower Mountain Mine under and beyond the golf course.

Later, it may have served as an air pit for the Baxenden Pits. A pump, marked on the 1848 OS map at the site of the present club house, may have had some significance.

ELLISON FOLD   SD704225
There were a number of shallow shafts and drift entrances to the Ellison Fold Pits in the Sudell Street area of Darwen. Although the workings by Brandwoods ceased by 1850, a brief, and by all accounts unprofitable, period of re-working took place during the 1870s. A circular shaft, lined with dressed stones and near St. James' Church, was the Chapel Pit of Brandwoods' Collieries. Little else remains of these early workings. The site of Coronation Pit, which was probably sunk in 1837, is now a car park on the east side of Anyon Street, Darwen. The Engine Pit, which suggests motive power, was situated in the Rose Street area of the town.

Extract from the *Report on Child Labour in Coal-Mines 1841:- Eleson Fold coal-works, township of Over Darwen. Proprietor Messrs Brandwood's. Number of males: 5 at 8 years, 1 of 9 years, 6 of 10 years, 3 of 11 years and 5 at 12 years. None of these can write, 17 can read, 16 attend Sunday school, 15 attend public worship. Number of hours worked: 8. Wages average 3s 3d, the highest 6 shillings and the lowest 2 shillings. Number of females: 1 at 9 years, and 3 at 10 years. None can write, all attend Sunday school, can read and go to church or chapel. The hours of work: 8. Wages average 2s 6d, highest 3 shillings and lowest 2 shillings. Young persons:- There are 22 males between the ages of 13 and 18 years, but no particulars have been returned. Number of adults is 39, no females. A large steam engine is in use, viz., 46 horse power. The ventilation is by means of shafts sunk in various parts of the mine to cause a current of air. The depth of the mine is 102 yards. The height of the gates or ways is only 2 feet in some places, and the runs are 200 yards. The quantity of coal drawn is three and a half cwt. The boys draw by belt and chain, the girls assist by thrutching. Carbonic acid occasionally makes its appearance, but the ventilation is said to be sufficient to expel it. No lives have been lost in the last 2 years.*

Blackburn Standard, January 1844:- *Richard Blundell was killed by a roof fall in the Ellison Fold pit operated by the Brandwoods of Turncroft.*

The same paper reports accidents to William Alston (19) and James Rainforth (9), in June and October 1844.

ENFIELD   SD746296
Opened by Joseph Barnes circa 1850, Enfield had underground links with Dunkenhalgh Park and Copy Clough Collieries. Also known as Dill Hall or Whin Isle, it was located by the Leeds and Liverpool Canal at Church. The site is best reached from the footpath by the lodge at Church and Clayton-le-Moors Cemetery. Follow this down to the swing bridge, but take the rough track on the left before going over the bridge. An area of disturbed

ground then marks the location of Enfield Pit. At the far side, within a fence, is the concrete cap of the shaft. Protruding metal girders could be part of the original headgear. The Geological Survey says the shaft was 396 feet deep. Part of a drained reservoir and traces of a tramway, which linked this pit with Dill Hall Shaft at the other side of Dill Hall Farm, can still be seen. Coal mining in Church ended with the closure of this colliery in 1883.

Blackburn Standard, December 24th 1856:- *H.U. Hargreaves, deputy coroner, held an inquest yesterday on Joseph Marsden, 48, collier, of Church. He and a man named Day were working in Joseph Barnes' Enfield Coal Pit on the 8th inst. about 7.00 a.m. It was Marsden's duty to examine the workings and to see that all was safe. He did this and said he could not perceive any damp. He then started work and immediately there was an explosion where he was working, about 6 yards from Day. Afterwards Marsden's lamp was found about a yard away with the top off. The lamp was not injured. Black damp had prevailed to a greater extent in the pit, and the lamps would not burn because of it. Marsden was badly burnt and taken home immediately and medical assistance obtained. He died about 6.30 on Saturday morning, but, before his death, he said he did not know what caused the explosion. It was so sudden he thought his lamp must have fallen over after he had put it on the ground. A verdict in accordance with the facts was returned.*

FIG PIE HALL   SD766272
Marked as a coal pit on maps dated 1784 and 1848, this pit was between Hollins Lane and Royds Avenue, opposite the top entrance to Haworth Museum. The area is now completely built over and it is not known who sank and worked the pit. However, it predates Ashworth and Hargreaves' domination of mining in this area and their first leases were taken out in the early 1800s. Fig Pie Hall appears to have been on the site of, or very near to, the present Haworth Museum. John Entwistle, who lived at Fig Pie Hall, was injured at Cat Hall Colliery in January 1867. A number of miners lived at Fig Pie Hall in the 1870s. They included James Entwistle and his son Richard, John Sefton aged 26, Richard Sefton aged 14, John Entwistle and Benjamin Ashworth.

FLASH   SD702239
The Brandwoods opened Flash colliery around 1845 to work the Half Yard Mine. It was worked by the Eccleshill Coal and Coke Co. in 1869 and abandoned in 1873. It was near Eccleshill Fold, Darwen, but little now remains.

FRIAR HILL - See VICTORIA COLLIERY (Baxenden).

GEORGE   SD775272
George Pit is marked on a map of 1784 and worked the Lower Mountain Mine under Baxenden golf course towards Meadow Head and towards Black Moss. Later, the shaft may have been an air pit for the Baxenden Pits. It

was in the triangular fenced area, now planted with conifers, on the lower side of the club house at Baxenden Golf Club. Nothing remains of the pit itself, though the line of a broad tramway embankment forms the boundary of the golf course above Meadow Head Farm, with another distinct branch heading towards the Edmund Pit shaft.

GREAT HARWOOD   SD735325
Great Harwood Colliery, now completely built over, was almost in the town centre, off Water Street and in the vicinity of Poplar Avenue and Maple Street.

Richard Fort of Read Hall, between Padiham and Whalley, sank two shafts to the Lower Mountain Mine around 1856. Numbers 1 and 2 Shafts were 200 and 110 feet deep respectively, and the seam averaged 3 feet 6 inches thick. The manager in 1868 was Thomas Redfearn of Russell Place, Great Harwood. Fort died in that year and the Birtwistle family and others then formed the Great Harwood Colliery Co., which continued to work the pit until abandonment in 1887. George W. Macalpine bought out the Great Harwood Colliery Co. in the early 1890s and traded as the Altham Colliery Co.

Accrington Times, September 5th 1874:- *On Wednesday at the county petty sessions, Blackburn, before Col. Bowden and Messrs Harrison, Bowden and Fish, two miners, Edward and Joseph Hope, were summoned at the insistence of the Great Harwood Colliery Co. for a breach of the colliery rules, and of an Act of Parliament. Mr Radcliffe prosecuted, and Mr Richardson of Bolton defended. Mr Radcliffe stated that the first defendant was charged with violation of rule 8 of the general rules. Sub section F1 stated that a competent person should be appointed for the purpose of examination of a place immediately before a shot is fired, and no shot should be fired unless it was safe to do so, and unless under the direction of a competent person appointed for that purpose. He was also charged with having in his procession a Lucifer match. Joseph was charged with having a key or contrivance for opening his safety lamp, in contravention of the Act of Parliament. Mr Radcliffe said that such breaches of the law endangered not only the defendants' lives, but also those of a great number of others. On July 8th an explosion took place at Great Harwood Colliery and, immediately after, the underground looker saw the defendants running away from its direction. He asked them the cause of the explosion, and they said they had fired a shot. That was their offence, because they ought to have sent for the fireman. The damages were slight, but the defendants were injured and suffered considerable pain from burns, though they had now been able to resume their work. Immediately after the explosion, Mr Tootell examined the place, and found in Edward Hope's pocket, a match, and in Joseph's an instrument with which they could unlock their lamp. The lamps were found locked, but the possession of an instrument to unlock them was contrary to the rules. Edward after admitted that he struck a match to light the fuse, and the explosion followed immediately. Mr Richardson suggested that, if the narrow escape from death and suffering which the defendants had shared would not be a caution to them, then no fine would be, but the Bench fined Edward 10 shillings and costs in each case, and Joseph 10 shillings and costs.*

London Times, August 6th 1875:- *An accident occurred early yesterday morning at Great Harwood Colliery, near Accrington, when John Standing and Jonathan Fleming, overlookers, were inspecting the air passages. They went down the mine at 2.00 a.m., but did not return. About 4 hours later a search party went down and the men were found to have died from choke damp. They were both married with children.*

Accrington Times, May 13th 1876:- *At the county petty sessions on Wednesday, Mr Radcliffe, solicitor, made an application on behalf of the Great Harwood Colliery Co. for permission to built a store-house for gunpowder. Mr Seddon, manager, gave evidence as to the nature and site of the proposed building, which is to be 50 yards from the colliery, and 200 yards from any residence. Permission was given to store 8 cwt.*

Blackburn Times, June 30th 1877:- *On Wednesday Richard Redfern had an accident at Great Harwood coal pit, when he was riding on a wagon laden with coal. It was being drawn up an incline by a rope, when the rope broke and the wagon he was in went with considerable force to the bottom of the incline. He was so severely bruised and shaken that he died the next day. An inquest will be held on Saturday.*

Although Great Harwood Colliery was not officially abandoned until 1887, the following incident might have signalled its end.

Colliery Guardian, March 1883:- *The Great Harwood Colliery near Blackburn is stopped through flooding. A miner working there last Thursday pricked a hole either into some old workings or a subterranean reservoir, and had to beat a hasty retreat. The other 80 men were immediately withdrawn, and the water has increased daily, filling up part of the shaft, although pumping has been going on since Friday.*

Accrington Gazette, March 21st 1885:- *Robert Calvert was killed on Monday afternoon, while preparing to come out of Great Harwood Colliery in the cage. After it had been drawn up about 3 yards it was found to be empty and Calvert was missing from the shaft bottom. A search party found him at the pit bottom in the sump hole, which contains about 2 yards of water. It is supposed that he fell out of the cage.*

HAMBLEDON HALL   SD790289
Connected to Brooks and Pickup's Cupola Colliery, the shaft here was 198 feet deep to the Arley Mine. Both pits were abandoned on December 22nd 1887. Hambledon Hall Pit is best approached from the King's Highway, a bleak and exposed track along the top of Moleside Moor. At a bend in the

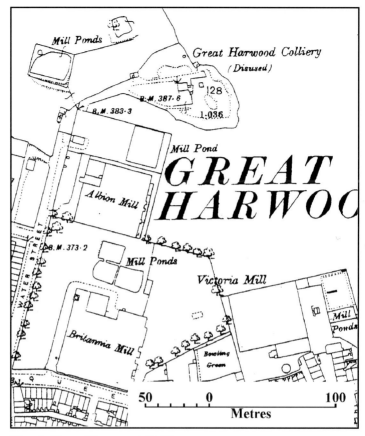

Fig. 7 Great Harwood Colliery.

track, just before the reservoir, a path goes up towards the ruin of Hambledon Hall. The remains of the pit are just over the wall. One of a number of spoil heaps behind Hambledon Hall marks the site of the pumping shaft. Further along the wall on the topside of the reservoir, and roughly in line with the tower and pier on the far side, is another shaft, brick lined and exposed a few inches at the top. This is in area of disturbed ground, and may be difficult to find.

HARWOOD'S   SD771225

Down Harwood's Lane, off the Roman Road at Hoddlesden, a road leads to Harwood's Farm. The tree topped mound, in the first field on the left, is an old coal pit marked on the 1848 OS Map. Harwood's Colliery was in the next field on the right, just before Harwood's Farm. The site is now marked by a mound in the middle of the field. Bits of colliery spoil can be seen on the side nearest the farm, but there is no trace of the shaft. The coal pit close to the farm appears to have been working in 1848, and two old coal pits were located to the west of the farm. According to Ann Stokes, a direct descendant, Joseph Place worked the Scotland and Harwood pits when he and his brother arrived in the district circa 1836.

HATTON'S SD708216

This appears as a number of shafts near Hatton's farm and to the north of Lower Barn Colliery. It was open by 1848 and seems to have been worked by the Pickups, notably John Pickup and family.

HEY FOLD SD689230

This pit, at the top of Dove Lane, off Blackburn Road at Darwen, took its name from the Old Hey Fold Mill, built in the late 1700s, and was opened by Eli Walsh circa 1858. It worked the Upper Mountain Mine at a depth of 345 feet. It appears in the *List of Mines* for 1869, but was abandoned in 1870. Little now remains.

HIGHER CUNLIFFE PITS SD701305

This large area of shallow pits, worked by a Mr Clark, exploited an outcrop of the Lower Mountain Mine near Bank Hey, Blackburn. Nine shafts, some marked old and one with an engine house, suggesting motive power for raising the coals, are shown on the 1844 OS Map. A nearby firebrick works suggests that fireclay was also mined here.

Blackburn Times, June 1st 1836:- *Last Monday while several men were working in Mr Clark's coal mine at Cunliffe near Blackburn, a large quantity of water suddenly broke in upon them and, before they had time to escape, they were immersed up to the neck. Fortunately there were no lives lost. Shortly after this, the earth above for a considerable distance sank about 2 yards and was instantly covered in water.*

HILTON'S (Messrs) SD682211

In June 1812, Samuel Crompton, inventor of the spinning mule, came to Darwen from Bolton and started a bleaching works in premises known as Hilton's Higher Works (later Spring Vale). Richard Hilton worked Darwen Paper Mills as an extension to his bleaching business around the mid 1820s. Paper making passed to Edward Hilton and Mr Walsh, while others in the family concentrated on the bleaching works and a new enterprise, coal mining. A lease, covering most of Darwen and including Rough Pasture and Higher Height Side to the west of the town, was taken out around 1840. A drift, marked *mouth of inclined plane* on the 1848 OS map and with an air shaft close by, was driven into the hillside at Rough Pasture. From here, a gravity-operated inclined tramway ran to the Paper Works on the other side of Bolton Street (now Bolton Road). In 1842 the coalfield was divided into portions, with William Pierce taking an area of Higher Wenshead. He and Eccles Shorrocks, of India Mill, opened a drift at Coney with the latter taking the larger portion. Eccles Shorrock also drove a drift at Dogshaw around the 1850s, when Hilton's drift closed. An engraving of Hilton's Paper

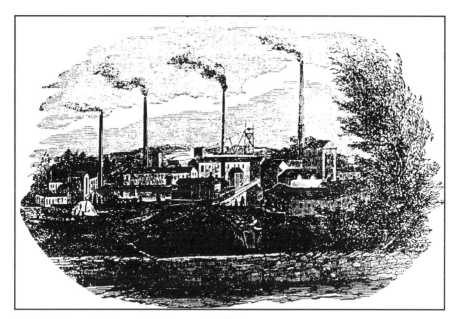

Fig. 8 Hilton's Paper Works and Mill Pit.

Works, dated 1877, shows a colliery in the background, and laden coal trucks in the foreground on a tramway.[6] This is Mill Pit, which was later used to mine stone for the new India Mill.

Blackburn Newspaper, February 1843:- *James Marsden, winder at Hilton's Colliery, Darwen, fell 40 yards to the shaft bottom, as he was descending to inform the underground workers it was time to finish their shift.*

HODDLESDEN   SD717222

Blackburn Times, May 15th 1932:- *Industry started in Hoddlesden when John and Joseph Place built the old Hoddlesden cotton mill around 1832. The hand-loom weavers at Yate-and-Pickup Bank slowly took to the factory system, though clung to their old homes and walked the odd mile or so to work. The population of Hoddlesden increased, reaching its maximum in 1861. In 1838 Joseph Place sank the Hoddlesden Collieries, hauling coal to the surface for over 40 years. In 1878 it was decided to use the fireclay under the coal and Joseph Place and Sons, sanitary pipe manufacturers, was founded. John Henry and William Henry were two of Joseph's sons and in 1892 they started the Ecclehill firebrick and fireclay works. Coal was still mined, but the whole output from the mine was now used to fire their own clay furnaces and the business became a limited company in 1897. In this neighbourhood the Yard Mine is 2 foot 6 inch thick, and the Half Yard Mine thins out at 14 or 16 inches, but both seams were worked on account of the fireclay that lay beneath them. Messrs Place employ some 350*

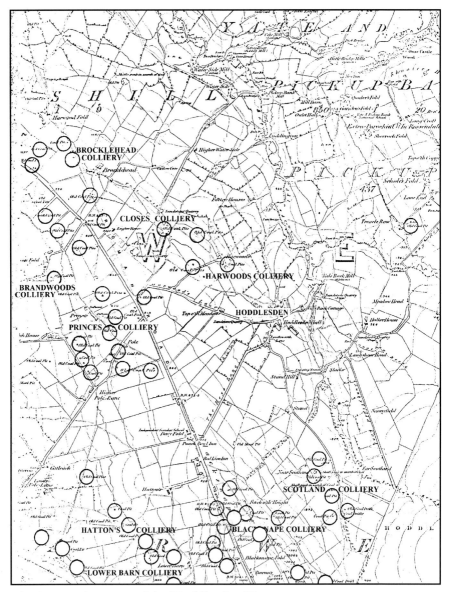

Fig. 9 Location map of the Hoddlesden Pits.

workpeople, and are currently sinking 2 new shafts to work both the Upper and Lower Mountain Mines and wind both clay and coal.

The 2 new shafts mentioned above were Place's Nos.11 and 12 pits, sunk on Hoddlesden Moss. They worked the Upper and Lower Mountain Mines, fireclay and stoneware. A chain road ran from the colliery across Hoddlesden

PLATE VI
Hoddlesden Fireclay Works
(By permisson of Ann Stokes).

Moss to the pipe works near the bottom of Queen Street, in Hoddlesden village. The pit also had a drift from the surface. A number of earlier shafts were at the pipe and fireclay works. No.1 Shaft, the oldest, was near Vale Rock Mill; No.2, the main shaft, was near Holker House; and No.3 Shaft, a pumping pit, was near Langshaw Head. These shafts, sunk in the early 1860s, were around 360 feet deep to the Lower Mountain Mine. James Ratcliffe was manager at Hoddlesden pit in 1896, when it employed 151 underground, and 21 on the surface.

A fenced mound to the left of the footpath behind Holker House marks the position of No.2 Pit. The location of No.3 Pit, in the woods directly behind the Bus Turning on Long Hey Lane, is also marked by a fence. Top o' the Meadow, or No.8 Pit, was sunk just before the First World War in an area previously proved by the Old Martha Pits, near Top o' the Meadow Farm, and was abandoned as exhausted in 1922. Its location is marked by colliery spoil and a capped shaft in the field between Hoddlesden Road and Harwood's Lane. Also on Harwood's Lane is old Sett End Cottage, former sett, or sales point, for Hoddlesden Collieries. The new Sett End was on the Blacksnape side of Hoddlesden Road, near its junction with Roman Road. The shelter, donated by Agnes Carus, was built over the chain road, which ran in a tunnel under the car park of the Ranken Arms and emerged at the Pipe Works near Graham Street.[7] To the left of the inn was a large archway, long since disappeared, which is said to have been a drift entrance to the mine. Some years ago, however, there was some subsidence in the houses to the rear of the drift mouthing.

Coal and fireclay went from the Sett End to the Eccleshill Coal and Fireclay Works till around 1938. The pit on Hoddlesden Moss (No.12) was taken over by the NCB's NW Division on January 1st 1947. A previously undreamed of luxury for the Hoddlesden miners was the installation of pithead baths in 1953. It must have been a bleak tramp for the miners in the late 1930s/40s across the moors each day following the line of the jig road, especially in the winter months, and it was not uncommon for the miners at Hoddlesden No.12 Pit to ride to the colliery on the coal tubs. This was against the colliery rules, however, and at least one man died when he fell asleep and was caught on the roof of the tunnel under Long Hey Lane.

In 1951, Hoddlesden No.12 employed 75 miners and 22 surface workers, with Mr H. Maden as manager. Fireclay extraction stopped around 1952, through lack of demand, and the colliery closed on September 29th 1961, through a combination of exhaustion and uneconomic workings. By then, the mine employed 99 men and its final year's output was 17,743 tons. The access road, built by the NCB, can still be seen below Pastures Higher Barn, and is now marked 'footpath'. Here, ten-wheeled NCB trucks took coal from the pithead to its customers. The filled pumping pit is fenced, and from the colliery site there is a fine view of the jig road. The site is now landscaped and, apart from a few traces of colliery spoil and shale, one would not know there had been a coal mine here. Hoddlesden Moss is a fine, but bleak, landscape and it is hard now to appreciate the hive of activity that once took place here both above and below ground. I was taken there in the depths of winter 1963 as a trainee from Bank Hall Colliery, Burnley. Twelve of us were left at the end of a moorland track high above Yate and Pickup Bank, with two picks and a shovel, and, as we set off across the moor on what was apparently an old ginney track, it started to snow. Our job for the day was to dig down at the side of the track and recover an old armoured cable. As we took turns at digging, the snow turned to a blizzard. All the trainees were dressed in pit rags, while the instructors had NCB donkey jackets, but soon we were all feeling the cold. We had no way of communicating with Bank Hall to tell them of our predicament, so all we could do was dig in and sit it out. The snow piled up on our frozen bodies as we crouched down, gathering what cover we could from the embankment of the ginney track. Then, around 2 o'clock in the afternoon, someone at Bank Hall remembered we were on Hoddlesden Moss and, as the only transport available was an open-backed coal wagon, this was sent out for us. Already suffering from hypothermia, we climbed aboard and endured the further indignity of being pelted with coal dust swirled up from the wagon floor all the way back to Bank Hall. As a result, 4 of the trainees were not seen again for 3 weeks, and 2 others packed in pit work the following day.

Blackburn Times, September 15th 1866:- *On Thursday a fatal accident occurred at No.2 Pit, Hoddlesden Collieries. George Adcroft, John Taylor and Ralph Sanderson were cleaning up their pillars when a large quantity of shale fell on them. They had previously tried the roof, and Adcroft, foreman, pronounced it safe about an hour before the fall took place. Sanderson had a narrow escape, but Adcroft was killed. Taylor was taken out seemingly dead, but a workman rescued him by breathing into his mouth. His injuries include a broken thigh, a dislocated knee and scalp wounds.*

PLATE VII Hoddlseden No.12 Pit (Burnley Reference Library).

Blackburn Times, October 11th 1872:- *On Monday Mr H.U. Hargreaves, coroner, held an inquest at the Ranken Arms, Hoddlesden on, Charles Welsh (Walsh?), 19, and Lawrence Nightingale, 34, who were killed at Joseph Place and Sons' No 2 shaft at Hoddlesden. On Friday they, with another man, got into the cage to be lowered down, when the shield with which the rope and cages were attached got unkeyed, and Welsh and Nightingale were thrown down a distance of 50 yards. Their bodies were dreadfully lacerated, and Welsh died instantly. Nightingale fractured his collar bone and died 6 hours after the accident, despite being attended by Dr Wraith.*

Blackburn Times, October 31st 1885:- *Mr H.J. Robinson, coroner, held an inquest at the Borough Police Courts on Wednesday on Edward Whewell, 42, collier, of 63 Blacksnape, who was fatally injured by an explosion of gas in Messrs Joseph Place and Sons' Hoddlesden Coalpit. Mr Dickinson, Inspector of Mines, and Mr Turton, Sub-Inspector, were present. Mr F.G. Hindle represented the colliery owners, and Mr L. Broadbent represented the fireman, James Taylor. Superintendent Myers and Inspector Noblett watched the proceedings for the police, and Mr Benjamin Holden was the foreman of the jury. The first witness was Whewell's widow and she said he was conscious until about 15 minutes before his death. She asked him how the accident happened, and he said that, when he had got about 2 yards from his place, he was lighting his lamp when it flashed up and fired. He*

61

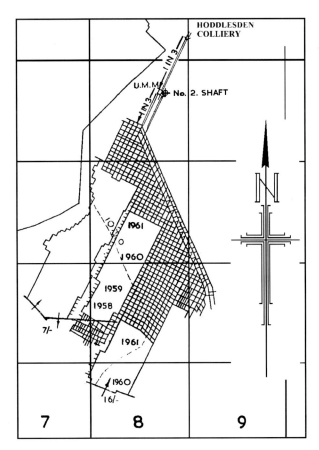

Fig. 10
Hoddlesden Colliery
Workings c.1961.

also added that he had met the man who should have examined the places, and he had said nothing to him. Peter Holden, of 40 Redearth Road, said: I am one of two firemen at Hoddlesden Collieries. I take the left side of No.1 tram and James Taylor takes the right side. On Monday we went down the pit together about 6.30 a.m. It is the fireman's duty to visit every working place on his own side before the men are allowed to enter the pit, under the third general rule of the Coal Mines Regulations Act of 1873. There has been no inflammable gas found in the pit within the last 12 months. Taylor was under me and had to report to me the state in which he found the mine. On Monday morning between 7.05 and 7.10, Taylor reported all safe, but I did not enter up the report until after the explosion. All the men going to their work pass Taylor and me at the wheel end and I saw Whewell go into the pit about 7.10. It is about 300 yards from the wheel end to where Whewell was working. I had noticed nothing when Shorrock came and fetched me to Whewell's working where I found him sat down, with Taylor, the fireman, standing behind him. I did what I could, then sent him home. The men in the pit do not work with lamps, but with naked lights. Whewell would not strike a match to light his candle when only 2 or 3 yards from his working place, for he would not be able to see without a light for some distance from his working. I asked Taylor if he had visited the place some 2 or 3 hours afterwards, and he replied that he had not been up Whewell's working, but gave no reason for this. Holden told Mr Dickinson that they examined the places with safety lamps, Taylor should visit 14 or 15 places and he visited 19 or 20 places, going the greater part of the distance on a sledge. It would take Taylor about 45 minutes to go his round of about a mile and a half. The places are about 2 yards apart, and it is the fireman's duty to put his lamp in each corner of the place and, if there is any 'fizzing' of gas, report it. Holden told Mr Hindle that he had worked there for 18 months and had never found a sufficient accumulation of gas to warrant him signing the book that the mine was unsafe. He added that he had always thought Taylor a very steady man, and thoroughly trustworthy. John Henry Shorrock, miner, of 21 Anyon Street, Darwen, said:- My working place was 2 or 3 yards further on than Whewell's in the lower mine. I got to my place about 7.15 a.m. He was going up to his place when I got to mine. He had his candle lighted. It was on the tub which he was pushing in front of him. I heard a noise directly after Whewell had gone up to his place and was out of my sight. I saw a little bit of smoke coming down his place. I put my candle out, and saw Whewell coming out of his place. When he got to the

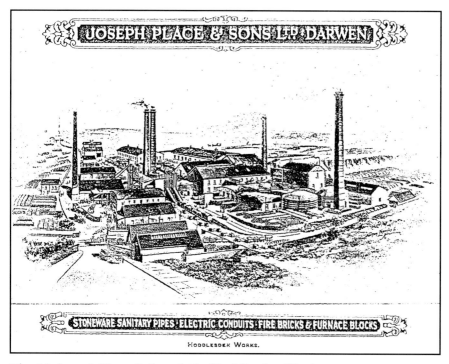

Fig. 11 Joseph Place & Sons Ltd - Hoddlesden Works.

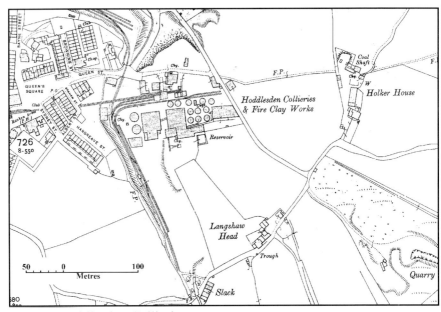

Fig. 12 Hoddlesden Collieries.

main airway he sat down, and then I went to tell the fireman who was at the
wheel end. In going to our work, Whewell passed the fireman first. There
was no mark in my place to show that the fireman had been there, but there
is plenty of air in my place. I have never seen any marks while I have been
there to show that the fireman had been on his rounds. I have never seen
any gas in either No.3 or No.5 places, and I have never seen any gas in the
mine. I have not seen any 'fizzings' of gas in the mine at all. Whewell
never spoke to me when he came out. Holden asked me to go for the fireman.
Shorrocks told Mr Broadbent:- I saw Whewell pushing his tub into the
working, his candle was upon it. I afterwards found his tub about 21 yards
in the working. He had nothing on but his drawers and boots and stockings.
He was badly burnt about the chest. He was conscious and could walk.
Whewell's candle was still upright on the tub when I went up to his working.
Ralph Taylor, underlooker, of Pothouse Lane, Darwen, said:- On Monday
morning, I was in the top mine, when I heard that Whewell had been hurt.
They came up for me, and I went down to the lower mine, and met Peter
Holden and his brother bringing him out. I went to Whewell's working
about 2 o'clock and examined the place. I could find nothing except a smell
of burnt gas. Peter Holden is responsible to me, and Taylor works under
Holden. I knew that the men were in the habit of examining the places, but
do not ever remember them putting a mark anywhere. They always reckoned
to see the men before they went in. I have never heard of any of these
firemen not examining the working places every morning, and I have never
had any complaints. I was talking to Taylor about 4 o'clock on Monday,

and I asked whether he had been in the place or not. He said he had not, but that was the only place he had missed out that morning. There is a firegrate in the shaft, but it is not kept lighted all day Sunday. The engine was not working on Sunday either. The fire has no effect on the ventilation in the lower mine and I do not think the steam makes much difference there. The lower mine gets a supply of air by a downcast and upcast shaft, no fan is needed. The steam goes up the same shaft. He told Mr Hindle:- I have been there between 12 and 13 years. In that time I have never known an explosion of gas nor found any gas likely to be dangerous. I do not remember a single instance when the men were not able to work owing to gas. He told Mr Broadbent that James Taylor had been there 29 years and had been a fireman all the time that he (Ralph Taylor) had been there. Lewis Bailey, PC 995 at Hoddlesden, said:- About 9 o'clock on Tuesday morning I went to James Taylor's house to make enquiries, after hearing of Whewell's death. Taylor told me: I went down the pit about 6 o'clock and visited all the places where the men are working, with the exception of the place where Whewell worked, and did not see the slightest sign of gas. I did not go into the old

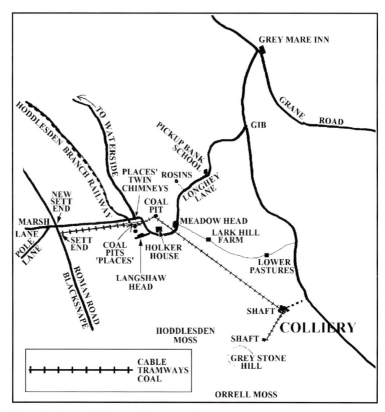

Fig. 13 Joseph Place & Sons Ltd -
Hoddlesden Collieries and Fireclay Works.

65

workings, but it is about 12 years since I saw any gas in the pit. I have been fireman there for 15 or 16 years. I carry my lamp which is a safety lamp. PC Bailey continued:- I wrote the statement down at the time in his presence, and afterwards read it over to him. Some 2 or 3 hours afterwards, I was sent to apprehend him, and did so in Darwen. I charged him with causing the death of Edward Whewell of Blacksnape, by neglecting to visit a portion of Hoddlesden Colliery on the 26th inst., whereby an explosion took place, causing his death at 7 o'clock on the morning of the 27th inst. John Turton junior, 75 Manchester Road, Bolton, said:- I visited the mine on Monday after receiving a telegram from Mr Dickinson. I found 'fizzings' of gas on Nos. 3, 4 and 5 workings on Monday, but did not visit that side of the mine on Tuesday. Mr Broadbent asked Mr Dickinson whether or not there was a great depression in the weather last Monday, and the latter replied that there was, and the weather was also very boisterous, which rendered caution all the more necessary. Dr Armitage said Whewell died from shock caused by burns. The Coroner, in summing up, said that it was the fireman's duty to go down and examine the mine before the men were allowed down the pit. The mine had been remarkably free from gas for a very long time, and the practice of marking the workings had been discontinued. He had been in some doubt as to whether a man for an act of omission would be liable to be charged with manslaughter, if any loss of life resulted thereby. He had looked at several cases, one of which was where a manager was supposed to see that the ventilation of the mine was properly kept up. He had had another man to do it and, because he did not see that it was properly done, he was held responsible. After retiring for about 5 minutes the jury returned, and the foreman said they had agreed a verdict of Manslaughter. He added that 4 or 5 of them were of the opinion that Taylor might have forgot to visit the place. At the Borough Police Court on Thursday, James Taylor of Hoddlesden was brought up in custody, charged with causing the death of Edward Whewell at Hoddlesden on the 27th inst. Mr L. Broadbent appeared for Taylor, and Mr Ramsbottom for Whewell's widow. The evidence given at the inquest was repeated, and no fresh witnesses were called. The prisoner was committed to the next Manchester Assizes on a charge of manslaughter.

Darwen News, July 13th 1892:- On Saturday there was a fatal accident at Messrs Place's Hoddlesden Colliery. John Duxbury, of 72 Sudell Road, was working in the mine when he was overwhelmed by a heavy fall of earth from the roof and it was only by considerable difficulty that he was rescued. He was taken home, but, although every attention was given, he died the same evening.

Darwen News, February 15th 1913:- Mr H.J. Robinson, District Coroner, held an inquest at the police station on Monday on William Eccles, 14, gig tenter, who was killed at Hoddlesden Colliery on Friday. Mr J. Cooper watched the proceedings on behalf of Messrs Joseph Place and Sons, while Mr C. Broadbent represented Eccles' relatives. Mr Gerrard, Mines Inspector, was also present. The first witness was Sarah Aspden, 8 Tithebarn,

Eccles' aunt. She said he started work at Hoddlesden Colliery about 3 weeks ago and this was his first job since leaving school in January. On Friday he left home at 6.00 a.m. and that was the last time she saw him alive. Mr Gerrard asked if he complained of his work and she replied that he was always willing to go. He liked the job and never complained of any risk. James Brindle, 12 Pickup Fold, fireman at the colliery, spoke next, saying Eccles was a hooker-on, which meant he had to see the pulling chain was attached to a fork on top of the empty wagons. At about 9 o'clock, Brindle found there was something the matter with the chain, so he went to see what it was. He found Eccles lying in the empty chain rut, and there was a tub, weighing about 2 cwt, on his stomach. The top end of the tub was up against the roof, which was 3 foot 6 inch high, and Brindle had to cut the chain to release the lad, who should have been standing at the side of the rails to see that the chain was put in the slot. The tubs went at a slow rate and so he would have plenty of time to put the tub in its place. To get where he was found, Eccles might have been pulling in front of the tub and caught his foot. He was then working by himself, but the previous hooker-on had shown him what to do for a fortnight. Brindle then told Mr Gerrard that when he reached Eccles, he was a few yards in front of a right-angled turn in the road, but should have been at the turn in case the chain became detached from the tubs there. Brindle had warned him not to go in front of the tub and there was a bell push for signalling to stop the chain in an emergency near where he was supposed to sit. The previous hooker-on had been about 15 and both bigger and stronger than Eccles, but Brindle told Mr Cooper that it was the easiest job he could give to a boy. Mr Broadbent commented that it was a very lonely job and lads did not stay with it for long because they were apart from all the others. Summing up, the Coroner said it was sad that a little lad with only 3 weeks' experience should be put to a job by himself without supervision. There was nothing to show why he got in front, but he thought that, if the lad could not lift the chain into the slot, it was possible he stepped in front to give it a lift, and had not got out of the way in time. A verdict of Accidental Death was recorded. Mr Cooper said that, to show their sympathy in a practical way, the firm had agreed to pay the funeral expenses, and any other similar expenses.

Darwen Advertiser, July 6th 1976:- Many Darweners speak of the tea-party in Hoddlesden coal mine in August 1857. Mr J.E. Place, one of the family that operated the pit, was also a teacher at the United Methodist Church in Darwen and he invited his young men's class to attend the party which was held in a 'room' 45 feet by 14 feet, varying in height from 6 to 12 feet, which was used to provide space for a bore-hole to prove a seam at lower level. Some 60 young men were greeted on arrival by another 60 young persons singing one of the songs of Sion. The men in the group of singers were dressed in black, and the girls in white. The room was festooned with coloured drapery and ornamental wreaths, while two rustic candelabra had been put up. Later, the visitors were offered a pedal or wagon excursion, then came tea, and afterwards a prayer meeting and singing with Mr Place at the harmonium. Finally there was a concert, and the inevitable speech making and Mr Place said he was willing to loan the room to any similar church party.

In September 1869, one Robert Hirst was killed in an explosion of fire-damp at Hoddlesden Pit. It was alleged that he was using an uncovered candle. Later the company was fined £5 and costs for permitting this, but Mr Place claimed he was not morally guilty. He said he believed that there was plenty of air in the workings. He also put the blame on another man, Nelson Marsden, who apparently had also been carrying a naked light, and said that, if he (Place) was fined, he would make Marsden pay.

The *Colliery Year Book* for 1935 gives the following information on the colliery and its owners, J. Place and Sons, with a Registered Office at Hoddlesden, Darwen. The managing directors were John E. Place, of Highcroft, Lytham Road, South Shore, Blackpool, and George H. Place, of Westfield, Lytham Road, South Shore, Blackpool, while J.E.P. Bury, of 48 Sudell Road, Darwen; F.R. Bury, of 99 Blackburn Road, Darwen, and H.V. Wolstenholme, Jnr. of Woodend, Blackburn, were directors. The mine was called Hoddlesden No.12 and was managed by Henry Maden. It employed 106 underground and 14 on the surface. It worked the Half Yard and Yard seams, with an annual output of 15,000 tons which were used in manufacturing. Both steam and electricity were used for power and there was also an annual output of 25,000 tons of fireclay.

HOLE IN THE BANK   SD774262
One of George Hargreaves' collieries, dating from around 1850, Hole in the Bank was worked in conjunction with Mitchell's Pit and the Railway Colliery, at Baxenden. During the mid 1890s, it employed 130 men underground and 34 on the surface, with James Whittaker as manager. It worked the Lower Mountain Mine, which here averaged 2 feet 8 inches thick, and the coal was used for manufacturing, coke and heating purposes. It was sent to Railway Pit on a ginney road running over the railway line and then distributed by rail. By 1900 the workings were nearing exhaustion, and the pit was officially abandoned in 1909.

The main shaft appears as a circular hollow, now filled with broken pallets, on land off Manchester Road. Workings connected with this pit included Black Moss, Browfield, Railway and Shop Lane (Edmund Street), but these connections were abandoned at the same time as Hole in the Bank. The latter is best approached from Hurstead Street. Continue down to the valley bottom and the line of the old railway, then turn left past the Railway Pit, a noticeable site on the right.

Accrington Times, September 18th 1869:- George Tattersall, collier, was charged with assaulting Christopher Kenyon, another collier. Mr Hall appeared on behalf of Messrs Hargreaves, Ashworth and Company, owners of Baxenden collieries, and asked that the case might be adjourned, as Kenyon was unable to make an appearance, as both his ankles had been broken and his shin bone splintered. James Cunliffe, another collier, was charged with assaulting James Rushton, insurance agent. Mr Hall said he appeared for Rushton who was a friend of Mr Hudson, underground manager of Messrs Hargreaves, Ashworth and Company's coal mines. Several disputes had been going on between the workmen and the managers, and the workmen had taken it upon themselves to leave their work. As the employers did not want to let the mines close, they had employed strangers, and the unemployed colliers had exercised great intimidation against them. On Thursday the 7th, instant, Mr Rushton had been to Manchester, and on his return home to Baxenden by the last train in the evening, he went down the turnpike road leading from Baxenden to Accrington. The night was very dark and, as he neared a quick thorn hedge, a man tried to get through, but stumbled against a stone. Mr Rushton then ran away, and the man ran also. Rushton then ran faster, but he was caught by the man, who struck him across the mouth. Rushton shouted out, and the accused said he had thought it was Hudson, not Rushton. There was not the slightest doubt, therefore, that the man intended to badly injure Mr Hudson. Rushton got hold of his assailant and, on taking him to Mr Hudson's house, found it was Cunliffe. The latter had also written a threatening letter to Hudson which Mr Hall showed to the Bench and which concluded, 'Hoping that something may happen to you, we care not if it is bad enough.' Mr Hall then said that it was fortunate for Cunliffe that the assault had not been committed upon Mr Hudson, else more severe punishment might have been the result. Mr Grimshaw then asked Cunliffe if he had any questions for Rushton. Cunliffe asked for the case to be postponed as Mr Nowell, whom he had engaged to defend him, could not be present that day. After some debate, the Bench agreed to adjourn this case, along with all the other cases in which the colliers were concerned. Mr Hall informed the Bench that he had been instructed not to apply for costs, as the owners of the collieries had no vindictive feelings, and only desired to afford their workpeople protection. Mr Grimshaw expressed satisfaction at that decision. The following are the cases which accordingly have been adjourned for hearing until next Thursday:- Thomas Clegg, John Hargreaves, James Margarison, colliers, for intimidation.

HUNCOAT COLLIERY   SD773309

This colliery closed on February 9th 1968 when the workable reserves were exhausted. The NCB colliery profile stated that: *Two shafts were sunk in 1893 to a depth of 276 yards, one for pumping and the other for winding. Both shafts intersected the Lower Mountain Seam which was abandoned in 1962. A new pit bottom was constructed in 1950 to the Upper Mountain Seam at a depth of 219 yards. This seam was developed in the late 1930s. At the time of closure there were 3 faces in production working the Upper Mountain seam, 2 in the dip district and 1 in the rise district. Two of the faces were fully mechanised using Anderton Shearer Loaders, which cut and loaded the coal automatically. The coal was transported in 3-ton mine cars hauled by diesel locomotives. In 1967, the production was approximately 150,000 tons, and overall productivity was up to 30 cwt per man shift.*

During reorganisation in 1950, the colliery's working depth was 240 yards to the Upper Mountain Seam, which averaged 3 feet 6 inches thick. Its longwall faces were 150 yards long, with electric cutters and conveyors. Sutcliffe gate conveyors and Distinction Trunk conveyors took the coal into a loading hopper, then directly into tubs hauled by diesel locomotives. Half the output went to general industry, and half to a coal-crushing machine on the surface before being sent to the NCB coke works at Altham. The coal at Huncoat Colliery was weighed in a cabin at the shaft bottom, with George Yates and E. Myerscough as the checkweighmen underground. This feature of the reorganisation raised output from 22 cwt to 39 cwt per manshift and the new cages held two 15 cwt tubs instead of the four, 4 cwt tubs held formerly. Shortening the winding depth cut winding time and so increased productivity.

There are few remains of Huncoat Colliery, but the bridge over the railway leads to the site from Station Road. The two infilled shafts are fenced and the line of the rail sidings can be traced. In 1896, 255 men were employed underground and 63 on the surface, with Henry Smith as manager.

Accrington Gazette, April 19th 1890:- An accident occurred at Messrs Hargreaves, Ashworth and Co's Huncoat Colliery on Thursday, when Thomas Chadwick, labourer, of 6 Back South Street, Accrington, who was carrying a plank on his shoulder along the tram line, ran against a wagon that was going in the opposite direction and was knocked down. The wagon tipped onto Chadwick's right leg, causing a compound fracture just above the ankle. His hand was severely cut, and there was a bruise near his left eye. He was taken to Blackburn Infirmary.

Blackburn Standard, October 8th 1892:- On Wednesday there was an explosion of firedamp in a new shaft being sunk at Messrs George Hargreaves and Co's Huncoat Colliery, near Accrington. John Loch, a sinker who was working in the shaft, had his face and hands burnt, but not badly. No other person was injured. The scaffold in the shaft was blown down, but no further damage was done, and the fire was soon extinguished.

Accrington Observer, June 15th 1894:- On Saturday afternoon, Mr A.E. Millward, mining lecturer at the technical schools of Blackburn, Church and Oswaldtwistle, took his students to Huncoat Colliery, and afterwards took them to the Victoria restaurant, Church Street, Accrington. He said they had visited one of the best laid out colliery plants of modern time, where the shafts were 16 feet in diameter and over 840 feet deep. The cages raised 4 tubs each time and could carry another deck holding a like amount

PLATE VIII *Canteen workers at Huncoat Colliery, c.1950 (Harry Tootle).*

*if necessary. Water from the pit bottom was wound in tanks attached to the
bottom of the cages. The cage conductors were of iron, 2 being attached to
each cage, while 2 hung loosely between to prevent all possibility of contact
when passing. The winding ropes were Elliot's locked strands with smooth
outer surface, which was generally favourable to even wear. The winding
engines were a pair of Cornish valves made by Messrs Robert Daglish and
Company of St. Helens. The cylinders were 26 inches diameter, stroke 5
feet, and the drum was 14 feet in diameter. The coal was passed from the
pit mouth by a chain arrangement on to the screens, where it was divided
onto 4 sizes—the fine going to the grinding mill to be prepared for the
manufacture of coke, the remainder going into railway wagons, carried there
by travelling belts. The ventilation fan was a Messrs Walker Bros'
'Indestructable', stoutly constructed, capable of running at a high velocity,
and discharging a great volume of air. It was 18 feet in diameter by 7 feet
wide, and had a double inlet, thus insuring even work on either side and
even running. The steam for the whole plant was generated by 3 Lancashire
boilers, 30 feet long by 8 feet diameter and made of half inch steel plates,
which provide a working pressure of 80lbs per square inch. The workings
were not yet very extensive, but the Dip Brow was about 1000 feet below
the surface, and, although the endless chain was only driven with a
temporary engine, it was a good example of this system of haulage. Mr Fred
Whittaker explained the workings of the compound and condensing engines
that drove the fan and also explained the screening arrangements and
mechanical appliances in general. Mr Nathan Haworth, a student at Church*

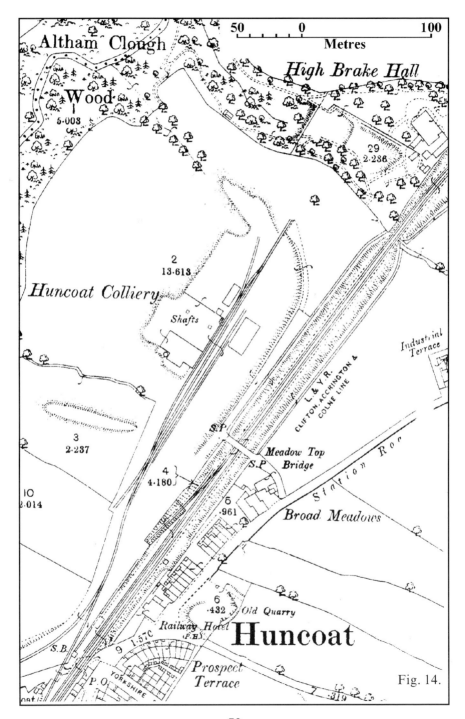

Altham Clough

High Brake Hall

Wood

5·003

29
2·236

2
13·613

Huncoat Colliery

Shafts

Industrial
Terrace

3
2·237

S.P.

Meadow Top
Bridge

S.P.

L. & Y. R.
CLIFTON, ACCRINGTON &
COLNE LINE

Station Row

10
2·014

4
4·180

5
·961

Broad Meadows

6
·432

Old Quarry

Railway Hotel
P.H.

S.B.

9 1·570

P.O.

YORKSHIRE

Huncoat

Prospect
Terrace

Fig. 14.

72

and Oswaldtwistle, gave a detailed account of the chain haulage system, while Mr A. Ratcliffe, another student, read a paper on mining matters, and Mr C. Gordon, undermanager at Huncoat Colliery, remarked on the changes that had taken place within recent times.

Accrington Observer, January 13th 1900:- *An accident at Huncoat Colliery yesterday resulted in a number of colliers being imprisoned in the mine for some hours after the steel rope attached to the up cage suddenly snapped, just as the cage with its load of full coal tubs reached the mouth of the shaft. With nothing to support it, the cage dropped to the shaft bottom, landing in the dip hole — a pit of water constructed to break the fall of the cage in case of accidents. The down cage, getting out of gear by the breaking of the rope of the companion cage, jammed in the shaft and cut off all exit from the pit. Up on the pit bank it was realised that to effect repairs would take some time and, meanwhile, the men would have to stay below, probably for the night or, as an alternative, get out by the air-way. The men were in no danger and cheerfully resigned themselves to spending a few extra hours below. Late last night it was reported that most of the men had got out by the air-way, while others were still waiting for completion of repairs to the shaft and cage.*

Accrington Gazette, October 9th 1909:- *Mr H.J. Robinson held an inquest at Huncoat on Tuesday on Thomas Edward Rhodes, chain road inspector, who was killed at Huncoat Pit on Saturday. Also present were Mr Roscamp, mining inspector; Mr Rhodes, solicitor representing Huncoat Colliery Co; Mr Whittaker, mining engineer; and Mr Kennedy of the local miners' association. Fred Whittaker, ginney tenter, of 23 Oswald Street, Clayton-le-Moors, said he saw Rhodes at work at 11.20 on Saturday morning when Rhodes was lowering some rails near his (Whittaker's) ginney. Shortly afterwards Whittaker heard a faint shout and stopped the chain. Going to see what was wrong, he found Rhodes about 3 yards from the ginney head, fast between the chain and the knocking off rods. The chain was underneath his stomach. Rhodes was not dead then, but he could neither speak or move. Whittaker sent for assistance, and Rhodes was released in about 15 minutes. He died a few minutes afterwards. Whittaker pointed out that the chain was between Rhodes's legs, suggesting that in striding over the chain he had been caught and carried back. He would have been squeezed until he could not breathe. PC McGregor said Rhodes's body bore a bruise from under the stomach right to the left shoulder. His watch was in his pocket, and had stopped at 11.15. The Coroner observed that Rhodes had evidently got used to his dangerous work, and in striding over the chain he was probably only doing what he had done many times before. A verdict of Accidental Death was recorded.*

Accrington Observer, June 4th 1910:- *It is often with a feeling of awe and dread that one thinks of descending a coal mine, and I must confess I was in common with the majority when I found myself among a small party one*

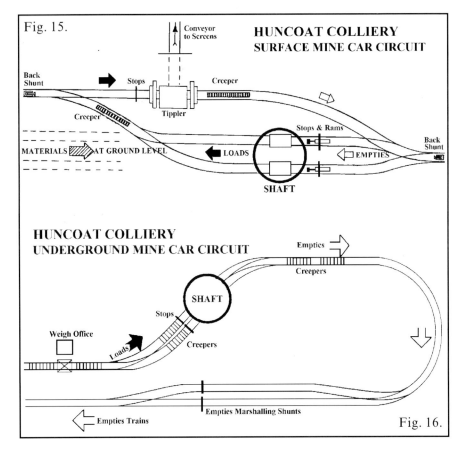

Fig. 15.

HUNCOAT COLLIERY
SURFACE MINE CAR CIRCUIT

Conveyor to Screens

Back Shunt

Stops

Creeper

Tippler

Creeper

MATERIALS AT GROUND LEVEL

LOADS

Stops & Rams

Back Shunt

EMPTIES

SHAFT

HUNCOAT COLLIERY
UNDERGROUND MINE CAR CIRCUIT

Empties

Creepers

SHAFT

Stops

Weigh Office

Loads

Creepers

Empties Marshalling Shunts

Empties Trains

Fig. 16.

evening a few weeks ago, about to go through the terrible ordeal. We set off for the pit head across the railway lines, and were soon turning the lamp room into a temporary dressing chamber. We were the each given a safety lamp and taken to the fan room. Here we saw a giant engine, the fly-wheel of which reminded one almost of the big wheel at Blackpool. It is continually going all day and night, and it is only still for about 12 hours on Sunday. We were allowed to go in and it was as much as we could do to stop ourselves from being blown down an immense well. From there we went to see the winding engine, then we went through the boiler house, and came out by the cages for our descent. I was in the second instalment to go down and I shall never forget it as long as I live. We had to go down about 900 feet, and seemed to set off as though the earth was sinking under us. Our hearts were in our mouths (at least mine was). The sensation was most peculiar, for from about half way we seemed to reverse the order of things, and appeared to be going up again. But soon we saw our pals waiting for us and we scrambled out and joined them. Shortly after the third and last load arrived, we began the important part of our visit. We had assembled in a large open space, and there was a small army of men whitewashing the walls and ceiling, and it was brilliantly lit up with electric lights. However, when we came to a small door in the wall, we were bundled in about six at a time and, at the other side, we found ourselves in a brick tunnel. Then our lamps were necessary, for it was the only illumination we had. We all set off up the tunnel, and the dust flew into our eyes terribly. In the tunnel, which was 1,000 yards long, we were able to walk comfortably, but after that the road got uneven, and the roof rather lower and many times I nearly scalped myself. We came to a full stop at a little station and, when we had rested for a short while, our guides decided to take us to 'No.4'. Off we started again, before long turning off to the right and through another door and there we came to a halt with a dead wall in front of us. Here, we were told, we were somewhere below Altham Church. Some of the chaps were looking round for coal, but so far we had not got into the workings. We then traced our steps a short distance, and took a turning to the left, coming across a lot of small trucks loaded with coal. A few minutes later and we had achieved our object, for before us was a solid wall of shining coal, and at the base a small aperture just large enough for the body to crawl through. Then we had to lower our dignity and slide gingerly through, and soon we were digging away with some most formidable 'toothpicks'. I did not stick it long, for it was rather warm work, and it is no joke lying on your back with pieces of coal filling your eyes and mouth, not to mention your ears. Then, as time was getting on, we started on our return journey. We came to a pumping station and here the lamps that had gone out were relighted by means of an electrical apparatus. On the way back we each had a pocketful of coal as a memento of our visit, and all wondered how we were going to get clean again. Altogether we had been down about two and a half hours, and we set off home in a merry mood. The experience had been a very happy one and each member was in raptures at having done something which thousands would never have the opportunity to do. Personally, being a Southerner, where coal mines are a thing read of, but never seen, I was in a very excited state. I sent one of my black diamonds home, only to hear it had arrived in crumbs.

Accrington Gazette, December 16th 1922:- *Mr James Whittaker, for 30 years the underground manager at Messrs George Hargreaves Collieries at Huncoat and Calder, was given a gold watch from the miners at a meeting of the Accrington Branch of the Lancashire and Cheshire Miners' Federation held at the Railway Hotel on Thursday evening. Cr Smith of Huncoat made the presentation, remarking that they were pleased to find Mr Whittaker recovering from his recent illness. Mr Whittaker had, said Mr Smith, always met the men halfway whenever they had approached him, and his energies on behalf of the workpeople, especially in connection with the doctors' fund organised jointly by the firm and the Accrington Miners' and Colliery Accident and Burial Society for the treatment of miners, were greatly appreciated. Concluding, Mr Smith expressed the hope that Mr and Mrs Whittaker would live long to enjoy the fruits of their labours. Mr J. Baron*

PLATE IX Huncoat Colliery - Pit bottom (Harry Tootle).

added that he had worked under Mr Whittaker for about 30 years and had always found him approachable. Differences of view had naturally arisen between them, in view of his position as secretary of the local branch of the Miners' Federation, but generally speaking there was always a close understanding and friendship. In response, Mr Whittaker said that he was glad to be among them again. He thanked Mr Smith for his kind references and he urged the members of the branch to endeavour to work hand in hand with the firm by whom they were employed. The conditions in the coal industry were difficult at the present time, but the prospects were much brighter than for some time past. Mr Whittaker also received a gold brooch. Mr Whittaker died on November 12th 1924.

Accrington Observer, January 13th 1953:- *On Saturday afternoon, Col. G.G.H. Bolton, MBE, MC, DL, JP, chairman of the NCB's NW Division, opened Huncoat Pit's £30,000 pithead baths from a specially constructed platform about 50 yards from a well equipped canteen in which the guests had gathered for coffee and biscuits before the ceremony. On the centrally-heated and canopied platform, in addition to Col. Bolton and Mrs Bolton, were the Mayor and Mayoress of Accrington, Cr and Mrs A. Brown; Mr J. Whittaker, colliery manager and chairman of the pithead baths committee, who presided; Mr J. Duckworth, president of the Accrington Branch of the NUM; Mr R. Lowe, general manager, Burnley area; Mr L. Plover, Labour Director, NW Division; Mr J. Hammond, President of the NUM Lancashire Division; Mr H. Howorth, Burnley Miners' Agent, who proposed a vote of thanks to Col. Bolton and the Divisional Board; Mr H. Whipp, President of the Local Branch of the NACODS, who seconded the vote; Mr J.M. Holmes, Labour and Welfare Officer, Burnley Area; Mr A. Bobbins, Secretary of the Accrington Branch, NUM; and Mr P. Riley of Mullen and Durkin Ltd, General Contractors. As a steady drizzle started, Col. Bolton cut short his speech, and the other speeches were made at the Odeon Cinema, Accrington. Here about 150 guests were entertained to a luncheon. Mrs Bolton was presented with floral spray. After Col. Bolton had opened the baths door, the gathering toured the baths which housed 432 pairs of air conditioned lockers, in addition to which a nest of 48 lockers have been installed for the use of men employed in exceptional wet workings. There are 27 shower points, and other amenities include water bottle filling points, drinking fountains, boot cleaning and greasing appliances, and sanitary conveniences, at both pit and clean entrances. There is a room for the baths attendant, and one for the first aid attendant, and an additional first aid room. Bathing and cleaning facilities already existed at the colliery for 138 men but, owing to the extensive reorganisation and increase in manpower, these were inadequate. It was therefore decided in December 1949 to adapt a disused engine and boiler house to provide as many amenities of a standard pithead baths as were practicable and work started on the project in June 1951. There are 500 men employed at the colliery, and the weekly output is around 3,700 tons.*

Accrington Observer, February 10th 1968:- Many employees at Huncoat Colliery would be filled with nostalgia as they left the pit yesterday morning for the last time. Our reporter talked in the manager's office with some of the senior officials at the colliery who had a long service and all said that on the whole it had been a happy team at Huncoat and they have all worked well together. The colliery, too, has not been without its moments of glory. Tom Finch, of Poulton Avenue, Accrington, the unit engineer, who has 41 years' service, recalled that in the 1950s the pit constantly hit the output targets, attaining a record of 1,300 tons in one day. Each time they did this, they were allowed to put up the flag and the flags wore out through being up so long. One of the reasons for the big output, he explained, was that whereas they formerly had 4 cwt tubs in 1950, they changed over to 17 cwt tubs, and then in 1954 to three-ton mine cars. The oldest serving man finishing at the pit is believed to be Tom Bridge, 15 Station Road, Huncoat. He is the storeman, and has had something like 50 years' service, including time at Scaithcliffe and Calder, though he has been on the Huncoat books all the time. Now almost 64, he started at Huncoat as a boy and at 19 went into the maintenance department, and then became a ventilation engineer. He has always lived near the colliery, because many a time Mr Finch, the mechanic, had to come in the middle of the night to wake him up and get his assistance, if something was wrong. When Mr Bridge started at Huncoat, his father, also called Tom Bridge, also worked there. They became known as 'young Tom' and 'owd Tom' and together they have put in 90 years' service at the colliery, overlapping by about 20 years, with 'young Tom' starting during the First World War. At that time Col. G.G.H. Bolton, whose family was associated with the Hargreaves in mining in Accrington for over 100 years, was away at the war, Mr Fred Whittaker was the agent, and Mr Jim Whittaker (no relation) was the manager. Mr Clegg recalled how for many years, after the annual Accrington holidays but before the colliery restarted, he had to walk from Scaithcliffe Pit underground to Huncoat, and then from Huncoat to Calder, as it was his duty to inspect the place before work began again after the holidays. As he was only 5 foot tall and of sturdy build, he did not find the underground walk too strenuous in those days. He said that, apart from a few months at Hapton Valley, he had always been at Huncoat or closely associated with it and he had had 47 years in the mining industry. Huncoat pit opened in 1892, and the second shaft in 1893. They are 70 yards deep, but mining in this area goes back to the 17th century. There are traces of mining on Moleside going into the distant past. This seam, known as the Arley Mine, was worked during the miners' strikes of 1921 and 1926. There are also traces of mining near Clayton Hall, and there are several old shafts between Huncoat and Calder. Coal was used for domestic purposes and usually mined by the local farmers. Later many pits were sunk to the Lower Mountain Mine. This was very good coal and was exported to Northern Ireland, but after about 1938 it became worked out and the Upper Mountain Mine was then exploited. When this was getting worked out it was decided to break through a fault to reach another stretch of this seam. This development was expected to prolong the life of Huncoat Colliery for a good few years, but, although there is still

PLATE X Huncoat Colliery - haulage road near pit bottom (Harry Tootle).

about a million tons of coal there, it has not been economic to work it. There are too many faults, and the coal has too high an ash content for today's market. That is the real reason for the closing of Huncoat Colliery, and is why the men accepted the closure without demur.

HYNDBURN COLLIERY   SD746323
This mine was behind the Hyndburn pub and seems to have been a drift, with an air shaft close by. The *Catalogue of Plans of Abandoned Mines* says it was abandoned in 1894, and worked the Arley Seam. Nothing remains of it.

JENNY LIND   SD762255?
Named after the Swedish soprano, Jenny Lind (1820-1887), it is difficult to say which of the Baxenden pits this was. It was managed by Richard Hudson, who also managed Railway Colliery. It may, therefore, have been the name given to the clearly visible shaft inside a dilapidated fence by the garage on Manchester Road. The coal was sent to Railway Pit, on a ginney road running over the railway line, for distribution by rail.

The Bolton family, who originally owned the pit, were great opera lovers and may have attended Jenny Lind's British tour during 1855/56. This may also indicate when the pit was sunk, but how Miss Lind reacted to having a coal pit named after her is not recorded!

Accrington Times, July 24th 1869:- Recently a dispute has arisen between Messrs Hargreaves, Ashworth and Co., owners of Jenny Lind, Wood Nook and Friar Hill coal pits, and their employees. It appears that the masters want to change a system of working which has been used for the last 50 or 60 years. The men regard this change as unfair, and have ceased work. By the previous arrangement, the colliers began work about 6 or 7 in the morning, and, having ascertained the quantity of coal required at bank from day to day, they hewed the quantity required and then went home. There were a number of youths aged from 13 to 17, employed as drawers, and each collier gave his drawer a proportionate sum out of his earnings. Sometimes the collier was fortunate enough to hew his day's share of coal easily, and so could often be done with his work before the drawer had filled the wagon. The young and more efficient miners generally finished work at noon or before, whilst the drawers finished about 2 or 3 hours later, much of the delay being caused by the comparative slowness with which the coals are sometimes brought to bank. The seams at which the colliers work are often from 25 inches to 28 inches in thickness, and what with the discomfort in the short depth they have to work in, the impurity of the air, and the water which falls upon them, and in which they often have to sit, the miners consider 6 hours' employment per day to be quite sufficient. The lot of the drawers is not so hard, for they have a distance of 300 to 400 yards in which to run with their wagons, and the altitude is comparatively great in one part. These youths earn from 9 shillings to 10s 6d per week, whilst the wages of the collier are from 16 shillings to 25 shillings. At

Wood Nook there are about 50 men employed, at Friar Hill Pit about 80, and at Jenny Lind pit 58. On the 7th inst. a notice was placed at the weigh office at each of these pits, stating that on and after the 12th inst. each miner employed at these pits was to start work at 6.00 a.m., or if later than that hour he had to obtain permission before entering the pit; and each miner had to see that his drawer conveyed the coals to the bank before he left the pit for the day, thus making it a duty upon the miners to fill the wagons with the rest of the coals he had hewed contrary to what had been previously practised. The men seeing that they would be delayed by this 2 or 3 hours later in the pit, without any advantage to them or their employers, expressed their determination not to comply with these conditions. At Jenny Lind and Friar Hill Pits the doors were closed shortly after 6.00 a.m. on the 12th inst. And, as the miners employed there refused to work in consequence, these pits are now closed. At Wood Nook, the men worked on Monday and Tuesday, but most of them refused to do so on Wednesday. Last Saturday, 15 miners signed a paper agreeing to work on the conditions laid down by the employers, and are now engaged at Wood Nook Pit, and the rest refused to comply, consequently about 160 to 170 men are out of employment. It is

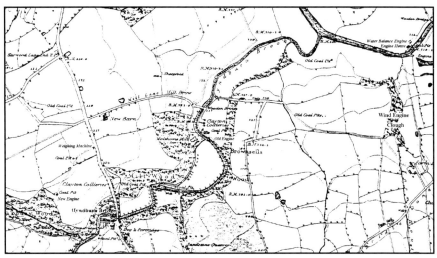

Fig. 17. The Hyndburn Area.

surmised by the colliers that it is intended to make one drawer work for two colliers instead of one, and thus reduce the wages for the youths. The masters have not yet made known the reason why the changes have been proposed, and the latter are suspicious that the object in view is a reduction in their wages. Six or seven colliers intend emigrating to America. The employers expected that on Monday the men would resume work, but only 3 or 4 complied. The men allege that it is tyrannical on the part of the masters to impose such conditions, and state that they will not begin work except under the same regulations as before. The colliers are not connected with any

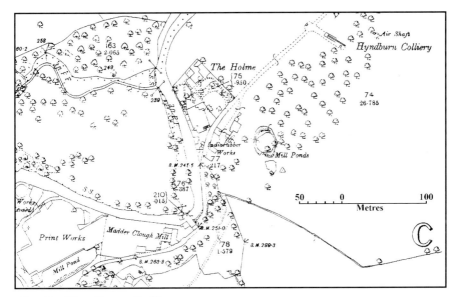

Fig. 18. Hyndburn Colliery.

trade union. In a circular which Messrs Hargreaves, Ashworth and Co. have issued to their customers, they complain of an unreasonable turnout of the men. The colliers have had several meetings on the subject, but no settlement of the dispute has, as yet, been arrived at.

Accrington Times, July 24th 1869:- *On Monday week, at 6.30 a.m., the gates at Messrs Hargreaves, Ashworth and Co's Jenny Lind, Friar Hill and Woodnook coal mines were closed against the men. A notice had for some days previously been posted up authorising the workmen to start at 6.00 a.m. and to remain in the mines till 4.00 p.m. A regulation like this, which compels men to be immured underground, in some cases for hours after they have actually finished their work for the day, can bring no pecuniary advantage to the employers, and is nothing more or less than a species of subterranean imprisonment alike intolerable to the miners and odious and repugnant to civilised society. The colliers are perambulating the streets, and are willing to work as miners have worked for the last 60 years, furnishing always a fresh supply of coal to suit the demand, which is all the masters have looked for in the past. This introduction of an entirely new idea has no value whatsoever, but will be found, if persisted in, great detrimental to the masters interest, deplorable to those workmen who have families depending upon them, and alike injurious to many branches of the trade which have an intimate association. A reduction in wages, which is an untimely occurrence for the workpeople, is a beneficent and merciful intrusion compared with this horrible interdiction. The men on every hand are unanimously of the opinion that it is purely the invention of Mr Hudson, the undermanager, who has only lately come into this neighbourhood, and*

81

in order to acquaint people of his coming it is essential that he did some thing of extraordinary achievement which contingency will transfer the business of the mines to others outside the neighbourhood, and in all probability his position as manager will be made singularly precarious. On Monday Mr Hudson closed the gates at Jenny Lind, and ordered the carts from Haslingden to go back empty, although there were plenty of coals on the heaps, and said further that no coals must go out that day. At 10.00 a.m., Mr Bolton, the manager, came and opened the gates and sent to Haslingden to inform the carriers that they could have coals as before. This event led Old John o'Margaret's to say that, 'He had been a carter for above 50 years, but never saw anything of the kind in his life before'. Mr Hudson lately came from a place called Boggart Hole and I must say he is making himself into an admirable scarecrow. What does he want to do? He wants to make a miner who can do his work from about 7.00 to 12.00 or 13.00 stay in till 16.00, doubled up, half starved to death with nothing to do save watching his drawer, who can do as well without him as with him. Besides, to start work at 6.00 means entering the pit at 5.00, as it will be a mile to the workings. Miners are entombed long enough already. They are an indispensable class of people, who make great sacrifices, and all are prepared to say that they well deserve their money. Why then seek to goad them by an additional incarceration, whose sole aim is human misery? Why alienate workpeople? Why sow the seeds of hatred, which only years can eradicate? Why seek to be tyrannical now, which will only be succeeded by months and years of repenting? Let Mr Hudson say. Yours truly, Live and let live, Baxenden, July 20th 1869.

Accrington Times, February 3rd 1872:- *On Thursday William Hindle, 32, collier, of Marle Terrace, Accrington, had an accident at Jenny Lind coalpit, Baxenden. He had finished work and was ascending the pit in a bucket, but lost his balance and fell down the pit. Fortunately he had only got about 16 yards from the bottom or he would have been dashed to pieces. As it was, he had no bones broken, but has received severe shock and internal injuries. He was taken home, and Dr Russell called to attend him. He is making good progress.*

Accrington Times, October 4th 1872:- *Isaiah Nuttall, miner, had a serious accident at Jenny Lind coalpit on Wednesday, when a portion of roof suddenly gave way and caught him. He was got out in a short time, but he was severely crushed. He was taken home and Dr Byles attended him. It is hoped that he will survive the accident, but he will probably be permanently injured through severe spinal injuries.*

KNUZDEN MOSS   SD720273

This colliery was on Brookside Lane, Oswaldtwistle, a few hundred yards past Brookside Colliery and over the brook. The site is marked by a raised pit banking, topped by a concrete shaft marker. In the mid 1850s, Simpson and Young sank it 85 yards to the Lower Mountain Mine, which was 2 feet

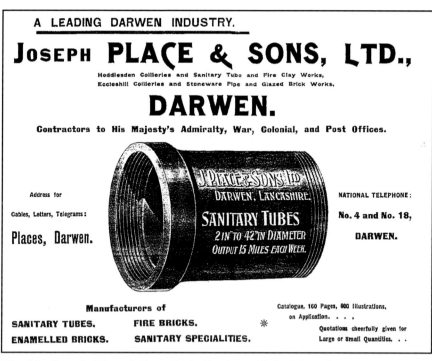

A LEADING DARWEN INDUSTRY.

JOSEPH **PLACE & SONS, LTD.**,

Hoddlesden Collieries and Sanitary Tube and Fire Clay Works,
Eccleshill Collieries and Stoneware Pipe and Glazed Brick Works,

DARWEN.

Contractors to His Majesty's Admiralty, War, Colonial, and Post Offices.

Address for

Cables, Letters, Telegrams :

Places, Darwen.

NATIONAL TELEPHONE :

No. 4 and No. 18,

DARWEN.

Manufacturers of

SANITARY TUBES.

ENAMELLED BRICKS.

FIRE BRICKS.

SANITARY SPECIALITIES.

Catalogue, 160 Pages, 600 Illustrations,
on Application. . . .
Quotations cheerfully given for
Large or Small Quantities. . .

Fig. 19. Joseph Place & Sons Ltd - Sanitary Tube Manufacturers.

thick. The men worked by candles, which caused a fatal explosion in April 1862. At first the coal was transported by horse and cart, but there is evidence that a tramway was installed later. A vertical steam engine, used during sinking, was later used for coal winding. The colliery was abandoned in 1885.

Blackburn Standard, October 10th 1855:- *Last Friday, John Hargreaves, coroner, held an inquest at Mr Davies' Commercial Inn, Church, on John and James Townley, James Hindle, and Richard Thompson, who were killed at Moss Pit, Oswaldtwistle. On the jury were Robert Wade (foreman), James Derbyshire, Hugh Catlow, Henry Bury, John Ellison, Robert Booth, Thomas Walsh, Walter Watson, Richard Taylor, Hartley Clegg, Edmund Walsh, James Whittaker, George Walker, Robert Warren and William Hodgson. Joseph Dickinson, Inspector of Mines, also attended. Thomas Duckworth, banksman at Moss Pit, but not acting as such on the day of the accident, said: I was there on Monday last, employed in filling the carts. About 13.03 I saw Richard Thompson, John and James Townley and James Hindle get into the tub to go down the pit after their dinner. When they had descended a yard or two, the rope started slipping, and the tub went down very quickly. When the rope became tight, it suddenly broke and the tub and the men were thrown to the pit bottom. We then got a new rope, and James Yates and Doctor Haworth went down and brought up the bodies. The rope is examined every day. I saw the rope on the vertical the same day and it appeared as usual, but I did not put it on that day. I thought that it was a little larger than usual, and projected higher than the frame of the vertical. I think that was the cause of the accident. I never saw arms - generally fixed to the sides of the vertical to prevent the rope slipping - upon this vertical. John Webster was banksman that day, and had the care of the vertical. The deceased had that morning begun deepening the pit. Coal had been got about 3 months. Duckworth then told Mr Dickinson that the vertical had been used for some time, but the wheels were made larger when they started getting coal. Joseph Haworth, the engineer, superintends the engine. It is his duty to look after the coiling of the ropes, but he was not there when the tub fell. Thomas Yates the engine tenter was there. Thomas Taylor, basket maker, of Kitchen Row, Oswaldtwistle, corroborated Thomas Duckworth's evidence, saying he went to Moss Pit about 12.30 and adding that the rope broke in two places. It appeared to be a strong one, being one and a quarter inches thick and four fold. One of the folds was torn from the other for 2 or 3 yards and about 25 yards of rope went into the pit. John Duckworth, George Haworth, William Entwistle, and Mr Thomas Simpson were next examined and they also corroborated the foregoing evidence. Thomas Yates, in charge of the engine at the time of the accident, said that he only came to work that morning at 9.30 after a week's absence. He did not observe any danger, or he would have given immediate notice. The rope when used for drawing coals projected above the ledge of the vertical for a full 4 inches, but he did not consider that dangerous. The rope had never slipped before. A verdict of Accidental Death was recorded, with the recommendation that the coroner should request Messrs Simpson and Young to cause arms to be placed upon their vertical, to prevent any similar accident, and that he should reprimand George Haworth, Joseph Haworth and Thomas Yates in order to make them more careful in future.*

Blackburn newspaper, December 18th 1858:- *Ralph Holman, collier of Oswaldtwistle, was summoned by James Baxter for the sum of 11 shillings, being one week's wages due to him for working as a drawer to Holman. Holman was ordered to pay the full amount, plus costs.*

Colliery Guardian, April 12th 1862:- *On Wednesday, Mr J. Hargreaves, coroner, held an inquest at Yate and Pickup Bank, near Blackburn, on James Brindle, collier, who died on the previous Saturday from the effects of an explosion which he recklessly caused in Moss Colliery, Oswaldtwistle, on the 3rd, inst. As there is a general absence of firedamp in the pit, the colliers are allowed to work without safety lamps and with naked lights. Brindle on Thursday week was getting coal in a place adjoining old workings which had been closed for 3 years. He had been frequently cautioned against the old workings, to prevent a quantity of firedamp which lodged in them penetrating the working part of the mine. At 6.00 a.m. on the 3rd inst., he was visited at his work by William Yates, the underlooker, who found he had made a small opening into the old workings with his pick. Yates ordered him to make up the hole with clay, and not to get any more coal from there. Instead, however, Brindle enlarged the hole and then went through it with his lighted candle. An explosion of firedamp followed, and he was seriously burnt on the arms, legs and lower body. His moans attracted the attention of Lomax, a fellow workman, who went to his aid and took him to the pit eye in a tub, as he could not walk. He was hoisted to the bank and taken home wrapped in flannel and attended to by a surgeon up to his death. He has left a widow and 8 children. A verdict of Accidental Death was recorded.*

LITTLE HARWOOD   SD703295

Some details of this colliery and its employees were given in the *Report on Child Labour in Coal-Mines 1841*:-

The children employed are 1 of 10 years, 1 of 11 years, 1 of 12 years. None of these can read or write, and they do not attend Sunday school or public worship. The wages average 3s 2d per week, the highest being 3s 6d, and the lowest 2s 6d. Young persons:- 1 of 14 years old, 1 of 15 years and 2 of 17 years. None of these can write, 4 can read and attend Sunday school, but not public worship. The wages average 4s.4d, the highest being 5s. and the lowest 3s 6d. The hours of work here are 8 per day, and no night work. No particular system of ventilation is adopted. Six adults are employed. The coal seam is 4 feet, and the heading generally 6 feet. The drawers use the girdle and chain. It is said to be a well regulated colliery.

Further evidence was given by Richard Ashton, the relieving officer at Blackburn:-

"At the only colliery in this district there are not more than about 8 boys employed, who draw the coal from the place where the men dig it to the shaft. The headings are said to be 2 foot 6 inches, and I think they work 8 hours a day. There are a good many accidents in the collieries generally, but not in Mr Clark's. I have seen the children come up, and have not seen anything in their appearance which indicates that their work injured their health. They generally become colliers when they grow up. The colliers are a low race and their appearance is rather decrepid."

The pit was abandoned soon after this (ca.1842) and is marked as an old coal pit on the 1844 OS Map. As Little Harwood Colliery is recorded in the *List of Mines* for 1883, however, it is likely that it was re-opened. It was then owned by E.M. Sharp, and Henry Smith was manager. After the following incident, the pit and a nearby row of cottages had become known as Blow Up.

Blackburn Mail, December 22nd 1819:- *Last Thursday an inquest was held at Little Harwood on John Landlass, Thomas Pilling, John Tithrow and William Wood (son of Mr Wood, boiler makers of Sheffield) whose deaths were caused by the bursting of a boiler belonging to a steam engine of a*

85

coal mine there. The explosion was tremendous. Fragments of the boiler were carried to a considerable distance, and the building enclosing it was completely dispersed. One man was carried along with a portion of the boiler to a field some distance away, and another, who was working in the Engine Pit, was killed when the stones of the building fell in to it. Three other persons were badly injured. One of them is still in a dangerous state. The boiler was about to be repaired and the explosion was caused by the steam pressure being increased beyond the extent of which it was calculated to bear. The jury returned a verdict of Accidental Death.

Blackburn Standard, March 3rd 1883:- "About 9.30 a.m. yesterday an accident occurred at Blow Up, Little Harwood, when William Bradley, 66, of Peacock Road, Little Harwood, and Daniel Hoole, labourer, were pulling down some coke ovens. Bradley died in the accident and an inquest was held at the Plane Tree Inn yesterday evening. There Daniel Hoole, who had a deep cut on his forehead and was very much shaken, said he was working with Bradley, helping him to pull down the coke ovens which were about 3 yards high. They had taken out a few bricks when the whole collapsed and buried them. He was covered in bricks etc, but he got his head out and shouted for help. He could not see Bradley at the time. A woman who lived close by came when he shouted and went for help. About half an hour later, she returned with some men who liberated Bradley and himself. Daniel Fletcher, of Bank Hey, Little Harwood, said he was called to Blow Up, Little Harwood, that morning. When he got there he saw Hoole partially buried amongst the bricks, but with his head out. They searched for Bradley and found him about a yard from Hoole, lying on his side. He was completely buried and was dead when taken out. He had a cut on his temple and some black marks on his legs, and there was about a cart load of bricks on him. The jury returned a verdict of Accidental Death.

It is not known when the shaft at Blow Up was filled or capped. Nothing remains of it now, but it was still there in April 1929, when it is mentioned in a newspaper report on two men accused of cruelty to an Alsatian dog. They were said to have beaten the dog with a stick and thrown it down the old shaft at Blow Up. When John Davies, a 20 year old moulder, heard of the incident, he went to the shaft, which was protected by a 16 foot high wall. Climbing over, he could see the animal's head and shoulders on a ledge 16 feet below, with its hind quarters hanging over an 80 foot drop. He entered the shaft and brought the injured dog out. It was exhausted and near death, but he took it home and treated it. It recovered slightly, but the next day it was too ill to take food or water. In the court case that followed, the RSPCA Inspector said the dog was, "*In a poor condition, unable to stand, and with its head swollen and face cut*".[8] It had to be destroyed, but the court complimented John Davies for his kindness and bravery in rescuing the dog. The owner, who inflicted the cruelty, was fined £5 and ordered to pay the advocate's fee and witness's expenses. His accomplice was fined 20 shillings.

Another colliery at Little Harwood was Croft Head, worked by Messrs E.M. Sharpe of the Little Harwood Collieries. It worked the Mountain Mine and was abandoned in 1888. Its site has now been absorbed into the industrial units around Phillips Road.

LIVESEY HALL   SD649262
This colliery was sunk around 1854 and abandoned about 1859, but *The Collieries of Lancashire in 1879* records a Livesey Colliery worked by Orlando Brothers. It was to the right of the A674 at Cherry Tree, Blackburn, but only a shaft marker and an area of disturbed ground now remain. However, the following suggests there was coal mining at Livesey before 1854.

Blackburn Standard, August 22nd 1853:- *An inquest was held last Saturday at the Duke of Wellington Inn, Waterloo, on Anthony Charnley who was killed by a fall into an old coal pit near Mr O. Brother's works at Livesey. The pit is used for draining the water from the clay-pits near the canal bank, and it was Charnley's duty to see that the machinery used to let persons down the pit was in order. It seems that something was wrong with this machinery, and Charnley, in trying to go down, slipped through the first scaffolding and fell on to the second. He had both arms broken, a cut under his chin and other severe injuries from which he died shortly after being hoisted up to the pit bank. A verdict of Accidental Death was recorded.*

The sale of Livesey Hall Colliery was advertised at the end of 1858, as follows:-

Blackburn Newspaper, December 31st 1858:- *To be sold by private treaty. The lessee's interest of and in the Livesey Hall Colliery, together with the steam engine, pumps, head-gear and the whole working plant. The colliery is now in work and is on the Blackburn/Preston Turnpike Road about two and a half miles from Cherry Tree railway station, adjoining the Leeds and Liverpool Canal and about two and a half miles from Blackburn. It is held under an agreement for a lease for 21 years, of which only about 4 have expired.*

LOL HOLE PIT (See Lower Darwen Colliery)

LOWER BARN   SD711210
Situated in the fields below Lower Barn Farm, off Roman Road, this pit was at work in 1848, being shown on that year's OS Map. According to the *List of Mines* for 1854, it was worked by James and George Shorrock. It was abandoned by the mid 1860s and no remains are evident.

LOWER DARWEN   SD711265
Mining in this area dates from the turn of the 19th century and took the form of shallow shafts. One of these was deepened by Simpson and Young in the mid 1860s, and became the Lower Darwen Colliery, also called Lol Hoyle (Little Hole?). The *List of Mines* for 1896 records that it was worked by the Lower Darwen Coal Co., of 1 Rhyddings Street, Oswaldtwistle, which was also

PLATE XI Lower Darwen Pit - (Blackburn Reference Library).

the address of Thomas Simpson and Co. They employed 190 men underground and 46 on the surface, with Lawrence Towneley as manager. The geological map shows two shafts at Lower Darwen Colliery. Immediately north is Simpson's New Colliery, which had a depth of 450 feet to the Lower Mountain Mine. Colliers at Little Darwen worked on piece, hewing the coal and placing it the tubs. The average height of the seam was 18 inches and it was often very wet, but the men could earn 3 shillings a ton for steam coal and 4s. 11d. for cottage coal. The underground haulage was powered by a steam compressor. On the surface, a ginney ran from the pit to Sett End, Shadsworth, and to a bank of coking ovens. Production stopped in September 1917, but evidence suggests that coal was taken from around the shaft pillar to fuel a large pump to drain the workings before it was abandoned in 1918 and the workforce transferred to Rishton, Whinney Hill, or Town Bent Collieries.

The site is best approached by taking the Knuzden Brook Trail from the cross roads just above the Knuzden Brook public house and following Knuzden Brook upstream. A large slag heap and the small reservoirs close by have been incorporated into the Trail, though the latter are not the ones that supplied water to the colliery boilers. The new industrial estate is only yards away and all traces of Lower Darwen Colliery may soon disappear. A capped shaft at Blackhill Farm on the B6232, almost due south, was connected with the colliery.

The exact location of the pit in the following report is not known, but it was one of many shallow ones sunk at Lower Darwen. It highlights the coal miner's hidden enemy, Black-damp, a mixture of carbon dioxide and nitrogen which will not support life, and which got its name from the fact that lights would not burn in it. Poor ventilation allowed it to accumulate. In this case, the man at the top realised what was happening, and resorted to the primitive method of throwing water down the shaft to encourage ventilation.

Blackburn Mail, April 19th 1826:- *On Saturday week, Benjamin Fish, who worked in a coal pit on James Wilkinson's estate, Lower Darwen, died as follows. The pit was some time ago closed up, but, a day or two before the above time, had been reopened. Fish went down to resume work after dinner, another person being at the top. When he reached the bottom, he fell and his companion, supposing him to be in a fit, called for help. A person who was near came and descended, but when he reached the bottom he too fell down. The man at the top, suspecting something the cause, dashed a quantity of water into the pit and then let himself down. He succeeded in bringing up the last person who went down, who in a short time recovered, but when he brought up Fish he was dead. An inquest returned a verdict of Found Suffocated. Fish was 70 years old and left a widow the same age.*

The following report of an accident at Sett End Coalpit may refer to Lower Darwen Colliery.

Darwen News, November 20th 1880:- *Mr H.J. Robinson, coroner, held an inquest on Monday at the Pack Horse Inn, Oswaldtwistle, on James Barnes, 35, collier, of 6 Kendal Row, Belthorn, who was killed at Sett End Coalpit, Belthorn on Friday week. At 11.30 a.m. Barnes was working with a man named Taylor, filling tubs with coal, when without warning a large stone, 9 foot wide and 4 foot broad, fell from the roof onto him, killing him instantly. Taylor was imprisoned for a short time and Barnes' body was recovered in about 15 minutes. The jury recorded a verdict of Accidental Death.*

Darwen News, October 9th 1882:- "On Monday James Aspin, 28, was instantly killed at a colliery at Lower Darwen when he fell 150 yards down the pit shaft. He went to his work at 4.40 to go down and examine the pit before the colliers*

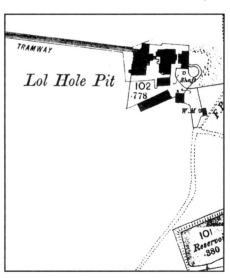

Fig. 20. Lol Hole (Lower Darwen) Pit.

were allowed down. William Brindle, engineer, usually in charge of pumping for the night shift, was in charge of the winding machinery, as the day engineer had not yet arrived. Unfortunately, when he started the engine, he wound Aspin up instead of letting him down, and Aspin, finding himself ascending, jumped out of the cage onto a sloping roof, missed his footing and fell back down the shaft, landing on his head. His lamp was afterwards found near the firegrate on the pit bank. Mr H.J. Robinson, coroner, held an inquest at the Original Guide Inn, Lower Darwen, on Tuesday. Mr Polding, solicitor, of Blackburn, was present on behalf of the pit's proprietors, and Mr L. Broadbent on behalf of Aspin's relatives. Mr Joseph Dickinson, Inspector of Mines, also attended. The evidence showed there was no banksman present that morning and the men, when they wished to enter the pit, had to give their own signals to the engineer. If the engineer had been in his place, Brindle would have acted as banksman. Brindle had attended to the winding for 2 years and, just before Aspin went to the pit, he had let John Pickup, a fireman, down all right. If Aspin had stopped in the cage, he would have been all right. Mr Lawrence Townley, pit manager, said he was surprised to hear that Brindle usually let the men down the pit as he had never before heard of him working the winding engine. The jury returned a verdict of Accidental Death, adding that greater care ought to be taken by the officials at the colliery. On Thursday James Aspin was interred at St. James' churchyard in the presence of a large crowd of mourners, including Mr George Haworth, manager of the colliery, and several of the workmen, together with the superintendent and many of the teachers and scholars of the Sunday school with which Aspin was connected. The Rev. G. Sumner, curate, read the burial service. Aspin, who was highly respected, leaves a widow and a child, and much sympathy is felt for her.

The reference to Mr Simpson's collieries in the next report suggests that they were on the tramway from Lower Darwen Colliery.

Accrington Times, December 8th 1883:- On Saturday Mr Anderton, deputy coroner, held an inquest at the Printers Arms into the death of Agnes Helen Hughes, aged 15 months, who lived with her grandparents at Badge-brow, Oswaldtwistle. Last Thursday, she followed her grandfather out of the house and was knocked down by some coal wagons on the tramway from Mr Simpson's collieries that goes through the brow. Thomas Wright, driver of the wagons, said he was driving 2 horses, each drawing 3 wagons full of coal, when his horse stopped. He looked under the wagon and saw the child fast under the first wagon. He had not seen her before. The jury recorded a verdict of Accidental Death with no blame attached to the driver. They recommended that a wall in Badge-brow belonging to Mr Lloyd be taken down, and that Mr Simpson's attention be called to the accident so that the drivers might be more cautious in future.

Accrington Gazette, June 1st 1889:- Richard Townley, 53, collier, of 54 Stanhill, Oswaldtwistle, was killed on Saturday at Lol Hole coalpit,

Oswaldtwistle. He was getting coal when a large block weighing about 4 cwt. fell, burying him completely and crushing him to death. A search was made for his body, but it was upwards of an hour before it was discovered. A verdict of Accidental Death was recorded.

LYONS DEN   SD674202
One of several early 19th century workings on Darwen Moor, west of the town.

MARSH HOUSE   SD703213
A small, early 19th century mine, in the Marsh House Lane district of Darwen, this was worked by John and William Pickup. Mentioned in the *Statistics of the Collieries of Lancashire, Cheshire and North Wales*, dated 1854, it was abandoned by the mid 1870s.

Darwen Advertiser, December 7th 1978:- *S.A. Nicholls, whose reminiscences throw much light on the Darwen of Victorian time, returned to the town after an absence of a number of years in 1856 and recalled, "We then took a house on Sudell road, that had been originally built by Eccles Shorrock for the minister of the Ebenezer Chapel in Bolton Road. This was the church that preceded Belgrave. It had a fine garden, with fruit trees and strawberry beds, in the area now covered by Victoria Street. It stood in the middle of a fold and had a right of way on sufferance only which enabled the family to go in and out via Sudell road. This road was built as a private route to Marsh House and Turncroft Collieries, and the only house actually in the road was the gatehouse at the bottom. The road was named after its owner, Henry Sudell of Blackburn, whose name also occurs in Sudell Cross etc. He was born in 1754 and became a prominent putter-out of work for the hand-loom weavers of the area."*

MARTHOLME   SD747334
This colliery was near Great Harwood, on the right of Martholme Lane. There is no sign of it today as the site was landscaped around 1995, but, during the groundwork before landscaping, one of the shafts was exposed. About 6 feet in diameter, it showed about 2 feet of single brick lining. The colliery was described as follows in the *Colliery Guardian* in 1895.

The winding engine, by Messrs Pollok and Macnab, has 2 horizontal cylinders, 27 inch in diameter, 4° foot stroke, Cornish valves: cylindrical drum, 15 feet in diameter, with a braking ring on each side. The engine raises 2 tubs in each cage, one above the other, each tub carrying 5 cwt. of coal. The winding ropes are of plough steel, one and a quarter inch in diameter, each fitted with a Bryham detaching hook. The conductors are steel rails, on the outside of each cage. The water is wound with the coal in an iron tank under each cage, which each carry about 1 ton of water. Water is also wound during part of the night. There is a haulage engine on the surface, with two 12 inch horizontal cylinders, and power is transmitted by a wire rope in the shaft to an underground road dipping south, 420 yards in length, over which the engine brings up tubs in trains. The remainder of the haulage is done by ponies. There are also self-acting jigs in operation. For ventilation one fan 15 feet in diameter, erected by Messrs Walker Bros. in 1887, is driven by one 16 inch horizontal engine. Quantity of air exhausted 25,000 cubic feet per minute, with a one and a half inch water gauge. A dynamo, driven by the fan engine, furnishes electric light for all the surface works. A cable is taken down the shaft, which supplies electric light at the shaft bottom, and a small pump in the dip is also driven by a motor from the same cable.

Over the years, there were several fatal accidents.

Accrington Times, August 7th 1875:- *Two men were killed in an accident at the Great Harwood Colliery Co's Martholme Pit on Thursday morning. At 6.00, when the men should have resumed work, it was found that Jonathan Fleming, head fireman, and Joseph Standing, dataler, had not come out of the pit to report all right and safe. This was very unusual and, after a short time, uneasiness began to be felt about it. The men were, however, ordered to descend the shaft, and wait at the bottom until Fleming appeared. They waited till about 9.00, but nothing was seen or heard of the missing men. It was then feared that something had happened to them. The men came back up the shaft and a search party was organised under Mr Booth, the underlooker. This party descended the shaft and, on getting into the levels, found that there was an unusual amount of blackdamp in the mine. They went very cautiously for about 800 yards, when they came across Standing's body in a place where the gas was so dense that, although Fleming's body was not more than 6 yards from Standing, over 2 hours elapsed before it could be recovered. There were no marks on the bodies, death being from suffocation some hours before. A crowd gathered about the pit to see the bodies taken to their homes, and much sympathy is felt for the bereaved. Fleming, 29, leaves a widow and 9 young children. Standing leaves a family of 9, but they are mostly grown up.*

Accrington Times, January 31st 1885:- *On Thursday Edmund Hope, collier, was killed at the Cock Pit, when part of the roof, about 2 tons in weight, fell upon him and crushed one side of his head, broke one thigh, and badly mutilated his face and leg. He was about 35 years old, and leaves a wife and a child.*

Rossendale Gazette, June 24th 1893:- *At an inquest on George Noble, collier, Glebe Street, Great Harwood, William Swales, miner, said that on March 30th he and Noble were getting coal together in the Great Harwood Colliery Co's Cock Pit. They were nearly through, when there was a crump in the coal and a piece about 8 to 10 lbs breasted off just as if a person had thrown it and struck Noble over the heart. Swales and his mate assisted him to a safe place, and gave him a drink of tea, and he said he felt sick. When he felt better, they dressed him, and they all went up together to the pay place.*

He told the inspector that it was not ordinary for pieces of coal to burst off and knock people over, but lots of pieces burst off when nobody was there. He told nobody at the colliery of the accident.

Rossendale Express, December 1st 1915:- *A fire broke out on Sunday night in the engine house at the Altham Colliery Co's Martholme Pit. The frosty air greatly aided the flames, and the enginehouse, which supplies the winding power, was gutted in a very short time. The drums, which are a portion of the winding gear, were burnt away, and the cages remain down the shaft. The Great Harwood and the Clayton-le-Moors fire brigades were called out, and a request for a hose was sent to Accrington fire station. At 9.34 the Accrington was taken to the scene by Superintendent Ware and 12 men to undertake pumping. When the pit is working, water is wound up in the cage, about a ton coming to the surface in each lift to feed a tank to supply the boilers for the fan engine. This source of water stopped as a result of the fire and so the tank had to be fed from the River Calder, about 800 yards away. The brigades worked at this through the night to keep the underground workings properly ventilated. The engine house roof fell in, and one of the walls collapsed, but the flames did not reach the headgear above the shaft, at some distance from the enginehouse. The cause of the fire is not yet known, but it is supposed the fusing of an electric wire might have been responsible. The extent of the damage to the enginehouse or to the shaft (caused by the falling cages) is not yet known, so it cannot be said how long the pit, employing about 400 men and boys, will be stopped. If the engines are useless and the shaft badly damaged, the stoppages will be considerable. Many of the mills and works in Great Harwood depend on Martholme for their coal. Fortunately, there was only one man on the premises when the fire was discovered about 6.30 p.m. and he was unhurt.*

Martholme Colliery near Great Harwood abandoned the Upper Mountain Mine in 1930.

MEADOWHEAD COLLIERY   SD730300
Sunk before1838, by Messrs Haworth and Barnes, the shafts at this pit are said to be around 390 feet deep, probably to the Lower Mountain Mine. Peter Wright Pickup, of Rishton Colliery, was in charge in 1882, when it may have been used as a pumping pit for Rishton. It was abandoned in August 1884.

It is found by turning left at the top of Henry Street in Rishton and was situated by Meadow Head cottages. Remains include a capped shaft, with concrete marker, and a ruined building, which is the staithe of the former clay works belonging to Adam Olive. The colliery access road has elongated stone slabs set at cart wheel width and grooved with wear. Stone setts between these slabs gave the horses something to grip on as they hauled coal carts up the slight incline from the pit-head.

Blackburn Gazette, May 2nd 1838:- *An inquest was held last Monday at the Cross Inn in Oswaldtwistle on Robert Taylor who was killed in Haworth and Barnes' coal-mine at Rishton. Last Friday he was repairing the pump tree which raised the water from the mine. A scaffold was hung over the mouth of the pit, suspended by 4 cords which were attached to the rope which was fixed to the jenny. Taylor stepped onto the scaffold to go down the pit. A man called Ward had charge of the jenny and, when Taylor got on the scaffold, he told Ward to let him down. Ward turned the jenny, and the scaffold went down and when it had got about 7 or 8 yards, Taylor called to stop. Ward tried to stop the jenny, but could not as it was out of gear. The scaffold went down rapidly and struck a trough which was in the shaft, throwing Taylor off. He fell 50 yards to the pit bottom and was killed on the spot. It could not be ascertained how the jenny got out of gear, but the jury returned a verdict of Accidental Death.*

Blackburn Gazette, May 29th 1839:- *An inquest was held last Friday at the Petre Arms, Clayton-le-Moors, on Ann Booth, 12, a drawer at Messrs Haworth and Barnes' coal mine in Rishton. On the previous day during the time when the machinery was stopped, she was leaning against a part of it when it was set in motion, and she was caught by one of the wheels and drawn in. The machinery was stopped as soon as possible, but it was found that she had been killed instantly. A verdict of Accidental Death was recorded.*

Accrington Free Press, February 19th 1859:- *Last Wednesday there was a fatal accident at Mr Barnes' Rishton coal-pit. Having finished work, Richard Whitaker of Alleytroyds was about to come up the pit when a stone fell from one side and killed him instantly.*

Of course there were disputes in the mining industry, such as this one between Joseph Barnes and his colliers at his Rishton and other pits.

Burnley Advertiser, February 18th 1860:- *Last Saturday at the Sessions Room, Accrington, before Mr James Worsley, John Smith, a collier employed by Mr Joseph Barnes of Church, was charged with leaving his work without notice last Thursday, along with 200 men and 300 boys. The whole of the colliers belonging to Mr Barnes's pits attended the Sessions Room to hear the trial, and marched from Church in a procession three deep. Mr John Pickop appeared for Mr Barnes, and the prisoner was undefended. He had been apprehended under a warrant, as the advocate of the working classes said that a magistrate had no right to issue a summons for such a charge. The rules of Rishton pit were that a month's notice must be given by the master or man before the contract could be determined between them, and that those who broke the rules would forfeit the wages then due. The colliers had formed themselves into a union at each pit, and last Monday they had a meeting to determine what should be done with 12 or 13 colliers who refused to join the union. It was resolved that a deputation should see Mr Steward, the manager, to inform him that they had decided that these men* should join the union, or the colliers would go on strike. Although Mr Steward received the deputation with kindness, he told them that he would not compel the men to join the union. The deputation, one of whose members was John Smith, gave him until Wednesday to consider the matter. A written document was given to Mr Steward containing the names of those who would not join the union. There were 7 at Enfield, 1 at Copy Clough and 3 at Rishton. The following Wednesday night they went to Mr Steward again, and he repeated his former answer. Next morning the men went to the pit top, but refused to go down unless their demands were met. All the men and boys immediately afterwards left the place, and had not been there since. The Act of Parliament said that if a person enters into his contract, and leaves work without notice, he renders himself liable to 3 months' imprisonment. Also they had forfeited all their wages, and many of them had a fortnight's wages due. Mr Barnes, however, did not wish to imprison any of them, or retain any of their wages. It was a great loss to him to have the works stopped, but it was greater to the men who had wives and families dependant upon them for support, and he suggested that they return to work, and all proceeding would be abandoned, and their wages paid as soon as they had settled down to their work. Mr Barnes always complied with their request when they wanted an advance of wages, but he would not discharge a number of hands because they would not join a union. The colliers had a short consultation at the close of Mr Pickop's address, but came to no definite conclusion. Mr Steward, the manager, was called and corroborated Mr Pickop's statement. Smith then made a long speech on human responsibility, starvation etc. and concluded by saying that the Bench could inflict upon him the punishment he deserved. Mr Barnes said all he wanted the men to do was to return to their work, and, if they would do so, he would withdraw the case. Another consultation was held among the colliers, and one of them requested those who would return to their work to hold up their hands, but no hands were held up. Smith was then committed to the Preston House of Correction for 2 months, with liberty to settle with Mr Barnes. A third consultation was held outside the court, when the colliers agreed to return to their work, upon which Smith was set free.

Burnley Advertiser, May 12th 1860:- On Saturday, all the colliers employed in those pits which have not turned out for wages received notice from their employers that after the expiration of 14 days the works will be brought to a stand. This notice applies to the colliers in Oswaldtwistle, Church, Accrington, Baxenden, and the neighbourhood extending almost to Bacup. A placard, bearing the names of Joseph Barnes and Thomas Simpson and Co. of Church and headed Advance of Coal Miners Wages, reads as follows - "Statements have been made at public meetings and otherwise, to the effect that the coal masters have advanced the coal 2s 3d per quarter, and have offered the miners only 6d, the coal owners pocketing the difference. Now the fact is that, since November last, we have advanced our miners' wages 22%, and they ask 33%, and including the 22% lately given, the wages of our colliers have been advanced in the last 12 years more than 50%, for the *same quantity got. During all that time the wages have never been lessened, but on the other hand, the price of coal has been very much reduced by the heavy competition, which existed up to last August, and part of our present advance in coals is only a recovery of the former prices. We now pay from 3d to 5d per quarter extra for carriage, and 3d per quarter at least for advance of wages to our other men, and have contracts to fulfil at very low prices, which, with the 1s 6d per quarter demanded by the men since November last, swallow up the whole of the advance on coals. The men speak of only asking 1s, not stating that they got 6d last December. They also omit to state that they have reduced our get since they received the first advance, thus increasing our standing expenses per quarter, sometimes to the extent of the advance given to the collier.*

Accrington Free Press, October 6th 1860:- Giles Sharples, 10, door tenter at Mr Barnes' colliery, was playing on the tramroad to Dill Hall coalpit on Tuesday morning. Around 11.00, he by some means got onto a wagon which was on the tramway and was found afterwards crushed to death. On Thursday an inquest was held at the Printer's Arms, Church.

Blackburn Times, October 14th 1887:- On Monday, Mr H.U. Hargreaves, coroner, held an inquest at the Roebuck Inn, Rishton, on James Ramsbottom, 17, drawer, who was killed at the late Joseph Barnes' Rishton Pit. Henry Clegg, a collier who had worked at Rishton for about 14 years, said he was working with Ramsbottom last Wednesday night and Richard Grimshaw let them down at 8.00 p.m. Halstead and another boy were also in the pit. Ramsbottom was drawing for him, and they were working all night. Between 12.00 and 1.00 a.m. some shale fell from the roof on to Ramsbottom and buried him. They uncovered his head in about 5 minutes, but it took about 15 minutes to release him, and it was about 6.00 a.m. before he was taken out of the pit. He complained of being hurt at the back of his neck. There was no one on the pit top, as it was not the practice for a man to remain on the top during the night when the colliers were working. The roof fell in the old workings. Nicholas Rishton went through the workings every morning. John Ramsbottom, of Hicks Terrace, Rishton, said his son had worked at Rishton pit since he was 9 or 10. William Kennedy, collier, of Rishton, said he laid out Ramsbottom's body. Mr Deaden examined it and said the spine just below the neck was broken. Ramsbottom died at 4.00 a.m. on Friday. Edward Pilkington, of Rishton, manager of the pit, said that Ramsbottom and Clegg were getting one of the pillars to increase ventilation. There was a space of 4 feet between the pillars there and the roof was generally good. He could not account for the fall except from extra pressure. They were not required by the rule to keep a man at the pit bank during the night. The jury returned a verdict of Accidental Death.

MILLERS   SD698206

This pit is marked on the 1844 map, in what became the Knowlesley Road/ Stanley Drive area of Darwen. It was probably sunk about 1815 and worked by Christopher Miller, but little else is known. The workings caused serious pollution to the River Darwen and possibly caused the failure of the Spring Vale Bleach Works.[9]

MILLERS FOLD PIT   SD759271

George Hargreaves and Co. drove this drift mine near Accrington in the 1870s to the Upper Mountain coal which was used in industry. It had a ventilation shaft at SD756271. Nathan Haworth was the manager and John Dewhurst the undermanager in 1896, when the pit employed 42 men underground and 5 on the surface. It was abandoned in 1923.

MILL PIT   SD695216

A capped shaft with a marker is all that remains of Mill Pit, sunk by the Hilton family around the 1820s to supply mills at Darwen with coal.

PLATE XII Mill Pit and tramway.

MOLESIDE COLLIERY   SD779288

This colliery is mentioned in several newspaper items in the 1870s and 1880s.

Accrington Times, August 28th 1875:- *On Thursday, James Hargreaves, 28, of Huncoat, was killed at Messrs George Hargreaves and Co's colliery, Moleside. With Henry Pilkington, another miner, he was removing some props upholding a pillar. The roof is rather loose, and a large quantity fell down and buried him. He was got out as quickly as possible, but he was dead.*

His body was taken to his home to await an inquest, which will probably be held on Monday as the Government inspector will have to be informed.

Accrington Times, March 29th 1884:- *On Thursday morning when the workmen went to Messrs George Hargreaves and Co's Moleside Colliery, they found the workings near the upcast shaft were on fire. A furnace is kept burning at the upcast and, as it had become too hot, the brickwork surrounding it overheated and set fire to the adjacent coal in several of the workings. Mr Arthur, general manager, was soon on the spot and attempts were made to extinguish the flames by bricking up the air-course. When this had been done, the mouth of the shaft was closed to diminish the draught. The fire had, however, got well hold of the coal, and in the afternoon the fire brigade was called. Mr Blundell, the superintendent, and Mr Ingham, the engineer, with one or two men, yoked 3 horses to the manual engine and went to the mine. A supply of water was found and the engine set to work, pumping water. A large quantity of steam soon issued from the pit mouth, but the engine was kept at work until about 4.00 a.m., when it was found that the flames had been drowned out. The fire engine was then withdrawn and the mouth of the shaft opened, but it will take several days to get the pit in working order.*

Accrington Gazette, October 17th 1885:- *The Moleside Pit Temperance Working Men held a public tea party and entertainment on Saturday evening in the Ragged School, Jacob Street. A good number sat down to tea and the meeting which followed was also well attended. Mr H.H. Bolton junior presided. A program of recitation, songs etc. was gone through, and the proceedings very much enjoyed.*

MOORHEAD   SD750296
This is an alternative name for Dill Hall pit at Church.

MOORSIDE COLLIERY   SD760324
A small pit in the Arley Seam, Moorside was briefly worked by Edward Pilkington around the mid 1890s, with 4 men underground and 1 on the surface.

Accrington Observer, August 24th 1895:- *Mr H.J. Robinson, coroner, held an inquest on Monday at the Hare and Hounds Inn, Clayton-le-Moors, on John Hitchen Pilkington, 14, drawer, of 138 Blackburn Road, Clayton-le-Moors, who died after falling down the shaft at Moorside Pit, Altham, on Friday. Mr Gerard, Mines Inspector, attended, and Mr Greenwood was foreman of the jury. Edward Pilkington, father of the deceased, said his son worked for him and left home at 7.15 a.m. on Friday, and should have returned about 3.30 p.m. About 11.40 a.m. Pilkington (snr) went to the pit to arrange about some pipes being cut in the shaft and, while he was there, he told the man who was working the engine to draw his son up as he wanted him. He then left and returned about 12.15 p.m. when he saw the lad laid out at the top of the shaft unconscious. He died about 2.30 p.m. The witness*

PLATE XIII
Capped Shaft at Mill Pit, with
Darwen's India Mill Chimney
behind (Jack Nadin).

told Mr Gerard that the man in charge of the engine was 21 years old next birthday. Mr Gerard then read the part of the Mines Act which stated that a person having charge of machinery must be 22 years of age. Witness then described the machinery over the shaft, saying there was a drum and a wire rope at the end of which there was attached a pulley, to weight the rope down. The pulley was seven and a half inch in diameter, and 4 inches deep. His son was pulled up by this device, sitting on the pulley with the rope coming up between his legs. He then told the inspector that there was no indicator to show how far the rope was going up or down, apart from a mark on the drum. The workmen went down the pit by ladders and came back the same way. His son was working close to the shaft bottom and, to come up by the ladders, he would have to go a distance of about 100 yards. James Edward Pilkington, 20, brother of the deceased, said he was in charge of the engine at the pit. He had not served any apprenticeship to engineering, but had had charge of the engine since it was put in last Whitsuntide. On Friday he called his brother to come up by the rope and, on receiving the signal - 3 knocks, then 1 knock - he wound him up. He saw by the gauge that there was more steam in the boiler than he expected and, when he knocked off the steam, the engine ran a time and his brother was drawn to the top and fell to the bottom of the shaft again. He told Mr Gerard he was also in charge of the boiler, which had a steam gauge, and, when there was not much work on the surface, he worked down the pit. Robert Pilkington, another brother, said that he was working along with the deceased close to

99

the shaft. He heard the last witness call for the deceased, and saw him go up by the rope. He also heard a shout and, looking up, saw his brother was falling down again. He tried to catch him, but the weight was too much and knocked him down. His brother had head injuries and was unconscious, and the witness took him out of the pit. Both the witness and his brother had gone out that way before as it was much easier than the ladders. A juryman thought someone was to blame for the matter, as there were Government inspectors to inspect the mines and see that the regulations were carried out. He thought that, if that had been done, the accident would not have occurred. Mr Gerard, however, said the juryman was mistaken. Every man was supplied with a copy of the rules of the Act, and every mine was periodically visited. He visited the mine in Whit week, and the rope was not in use, and the men were using the ladder. With regards to Acts of Parliament, the pit was worked in a casual way. A verdict of Accidental Death was recorded.

OLD LYONS   SD676191

John Tattersall, who had links with other collieries in the Oswaldtwistle district, leased the pit in the early 1830s. He went bankrupt in 1844, but the mine was worked by partners Robert Scholes and Nicholas Fish in 1854, when it was listed in *Statistics of the Collieries of Lancashire, Cheshire and North Wales*. Fish and Holden had it in 1869. Mining stopped in the 1870s when the seams were exhausted. There is evidence, however, that Ralph Brownlow, of Hollins Head Terrace, Tockholes, briefly reopened the pit around 1895. He worked the Lower Mountain Mine, with 3 men underground and 2 on the surface. Coal Pit Lane is probably named after Old Lyons Colliery. A capped shaft and a number of engine beds, along with a ruined winding house, mark the site today.

Extract from the *Report on Child Labour in Coal-Mines 1841*:- *Mr John Tattersall, Old Lions Colliery, Over Darwen, parish of Blackburn. Children under 13 years: 2 at 9 years, 2 at 10 years and 3 of 11 years. Young persons: 1 of 13 years, 2 of 14 years, 1 of 15 years and 1 of 16. They are paid by quantity not time, hours of work being 10 per day. Females: 1 girl aged 14 years whose wage is 5s. per week, hours of work same as males. The workmen descend the mine by a shaft 20 yards deep, and are let down by one of the above ground men. Only one workman is allowed to descend at each turn. No accident has occurred for the last 2 years. The gates or roads are 2 feet 3 inches high, the runs 65 to 70 yards. The weight of coal brought by the drawers is about 150 lbs. They draw by the belt and chain. No firedamp is found here. The men are forbidden to strike the children. No school or sick-fund, but the book-keeper teaches the children to read. Number of adults employed, 10 males.*

POLE PIT   SD703213

In 1869 William Pickup worked this pit at Marsh House. It is also called Pole Lane Colliery.

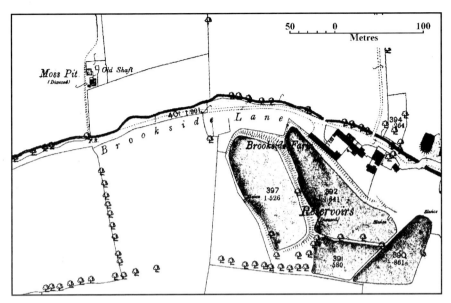

Fig. 21. *Moss Pit.*

Blackburn Newspaper, December 1838:- *Last Saturday some boys were amusing themselves by playing around in James Pickup's coalpit when part of the roof fell in. One boy, Thomas Entwistle, was buried and, when taken out, he was dead. An inquest will be held today.*

Blackburn Standard, January 26th 1859:- *John Waterhouse, 15, was killed last Friday in John Pickup's pit, Marsh House Lane, Over Darwen. He was filling a tub, when a portion of roof fell and suffocated him. An inquest returned a verdict of Accidental Death.*

Accrington Times, June 26th 1869:- *Thomas Harwood, 13, died after falling 12 yards down the shaft of an old coal pit which was being re-opened to provide a draught of air to Pole Lane Colliery. A verdict of Accidental Death was recorded.*

PRINCES   SD707224

Near the top of Marsh House Lane, Darwen, a lane on the left leads to the ruins of Princes Farm. The area between Ellison Fold Lane, Roman Road and Marsh House Lane has been extensively worked, mostly during the 1830s and 1840s. Princes Colliery was on the left of the track, near the farm, and is shown on the 1848 OS Map. Six old coal pits and 4 coal pits, which were presumably working, are marked on this map, but there is little other information on them. A number of small spoil heaps can be seen beyond the old farm. Also near it are some large blocks of stone. Too large for the farm structure, they may be engine beds, or stone work from an engine house.

Prince Colliery, Eccleshill, is listed as standing in the *List of Mines* for 1879, when W. Pickup of Star Street, Darwen, was the owner. This is probably the same William Pickup who, with John Pickup, worked the Pole, and the nearby Marsh House Colliery.

RAILWAY PIT   SD772262
This drift, which connected with Jenny Lind Pit, was between Manchester Road and Hurststead. The Upper and Lower Mountain Mines were both worked, the former being 2 foot thick and the latter averaging 2 foot 6 inches. One of George Hargreaves' pits, it dates from around the 1850s. Mining stopped in 1894, but the drift was kept open to ventilate Hole in the Bank Colliery.

A more important site, connected with the Railway Pit, is reached by the lane by Baxenden Conservative Club. On the left, above the former railway line, are two walled up drift mine entrances (one of which may be the Dewhurst Drift), behind which is a large, stone, retaining wall. There was a large bank of coke ovens here, and water from the lodge above the site at the bottom of Tom Dule Clough was probably used to quench the coke. Further along the bed of the main railway line is the embankment of the colliery sidings. A tramway went from here to the shaft on Manchester Road.

In November 1866, two tramps were brought before the Sessions Room at Accrington, charged with having no fixed abode. PC Ormes said that on the previous Saturday night he was told that two men were asleep in Messrs Ashworth and Hargreaves' cinder (coke) ovens. On investigation he found the two men, one without his hat and stockings. They told him they had nowhere to go. Each had one penny on his person. He told the Sessions that both men were fit and able and, after due consideration, they were gaoled for 21 days with hard labour.

Accrington Times, April 31st 1870:- *James Hindle, 36, collier, died on Wednesday afternoon following an explosion in Messrs Hargreaves and Ashworth and Co's Railway Pit, Baxenden, The original shaft at this pit was sunk many years ago, and coal has been taken from the workings until recently, when the coal became exhausted. A new shaft was sunk some 36 yards lower down, and workings started on this level. From the plan, these new workings are ventilated by means of an air pipe about a foot in diameter which is carried from the top of the original shaft and connected with the workings of the new level by means of a trunk at the bottom of the new shaft. The air pipe stretches a few yards within the workings. To the left of the bottom of the new shaft a lodge is being built to hold the water until means be found to remove it from the pit. Further on, in the direction of the air pipe, is the principal roadway, which has been carried on for about 170 yards, until the dangerous appearance of water caused the workings to be stopped. To block the way to this part of the level, a brick wall has been erected across the road a little way beyond the mouth of the air pipe, which*

PLATE XIV Drift entrance at Railway Pit, Baxenden (Jack Nadin).

has only been carried a few yards into the workings, and has not passed the wall. On the left, 6 yards from the shaft bottom and a little beyond the termination of the air pipe, a new drift has been started. Hindle and William Whittaker had worked in the water lodge all day on Tuesday. Two more colliers, Clegg and Kenyon, had worked in the new drift on the left, about 6 yards from the former place. At 13.00, Hindle, wanting a spade, went to the drift where Clegg and Kenyon had been at work with a naked candle and, just as he was leaving, the explosion took place, carrying him with great force down the road and hurling bricks from the wall behind on to him. He was driven along with the debris from the workings and the sides of the pit which struck him at the shaft bottom. Fortunately Whittaker heard the rattle of the explosion and laid himself flat on the ground, and was thus only slightly injured. After the explosion, Whittaker was drawn up the shaft but, on not seeing his companion, he went straight back down before the after-damp was formed and found Hindle lying senseless with his skull cut open and other parts of his body burnt and injured. Both men were drawn up, and Hindle was conveyed home to be attended by Dr Russell, but he died that afternoon, leaving a wife and 3 children. His death has also caused much grief among his associates. The cause of the explosion is not known. First it was thought an accumulation of gas behind the brick wall may have penetrated into the drift and not been sufficiently rarefied by the air from the air pipe. But only 2 hours before the explosion, Clegg and Kenyon, both experienced miners, had felt all to be safe in this respect, and Mr

103

Hudson, pit manager, had examined all the workings that morning and found all in a safe condition. The trunk or air pipe was found to be injured, having a tendency to stop the full supply of air, but whether the explosion was caused by this deficiency in the ventilation cannot be said.

At the inquest in late April, the jury reached the following verdict: *We are of the opinion that this is Accidental Death through stopping the ventilation in the main drift by disconnecting the air pipes. We are of the opinion that this ought never to have been allowed. We also think the manager is to blame for not appointing a competent fireman after the first explosion.*

Richard Hudson, the manager at the colliery, was not impressed with the outcome of the inquest, and saw fit to write to the editor of the *Accrington Times*, outlining his case.

Accrington Times, May 7th 1870:- *...The inquiry has left the matter in a very unsatisfactory and unfair position, as regards myself, the jury's verdict being that the disconnection of the air pipes ought not to have been allowed, and that a fireman ought to have been appointed after February 16th, when a slight explosion occurred. From the first time gas was detected, while the pit was being sunk, I have watched the place carefully and, when the slight explosion took place, I insisted that the underlooker should go on no longer with the ventilation as it then stood, and he then by my directions put in a 12 inch air pipe in place of the former 6 inch pipes. There were only 2 men working in the pit at a time, and I gave them safety lamps to test the place every morning, and I gave the keys to the engineman, with strict orders to see the lamps locked every morning before they were taken down to test the place. This was the underlooker's duty, but, to make sure, I did it myself and made frequent enquiries if gas could be detected, but was always answered in the negative. Nothing could possibly be more perfect than the ventilation in this pit during the 9 weeks which elapsed from February 16th to April 20th when the pipes were disconnected, for in this time no trace of gas was found. The ventilation was so complete that the men had disregarded the orders I had given them, and without my knowledge had gone down without safety lamps. The underlooker was also misled by this into concluding that no gas existed and so, after disconnecting the air pipes, during the after part of the day he omitted testing the place where the ventilation had been suspended. His confidence that no gas was being made also led him to leave the pit without plastering up the stopping. Had this been done, it would have prevented gas igniting in the drift beyond it. It was an error of judgement on his part. I was away all that day, but I always found him to be an intelligent and vigilant man, and, therefore, placed great reliance upon him. The ventilation was perfect, and indeed excessive, and to appoint a fireman in these circumstances, at a new pit, where only 2 men were working was quite unnecessary, the underlooker being quite competent to perform the duty, which was at most a nominal one. But a fireman would not have prevented the accident. The place was quite clear when the*

104

underlooker went in the morning, and the visit of a fireman would have been useless. No-one can regret the occurrence more than I do, but I must in fairness to myself bring out the true state of the case. I am locally unpopular because of certain alterations which I have made at the pits, and it was evident (to me at least) that the jury were determined to throw all the blame on me, and they succeeded in their efforts. Yours obediently. Richard Hudson, Baxenden, May 4th 1870.

In May, however, George Smith, the underlooker at the colliery, was charged with neglect.

Accrington Times, May 21st 1870:- George Smith, a middle-aged man employed as underlooker at Baxenden Colliery, was charged with infringing the 32nd special rule which required that when firedamp had been found in any of the shafts or workings the underlooker should examine, and appoint a fireman to, that part of the workings under his charge. He was also charged with violating the 33rd special rule, requiring the underlooker to maintain adequate ventilation. George Smith was summoned by Mr Dickinson, Inspector of Mines. On being charged with the offences, he said he was at Cathole and could not be in both places at once. He added that appointing a fireman had always been considered the duty of the master or manager at Baxenden Colliery. Mr Ashworth, the Clerk, asked about ventilation and Smith said it was good from February 16th to April 15th. He was not much acquainted with gas, however, and, when the pipes were disconnected on the 19th, he could not put them across. Mr Holden, solicitor, of Bolton, appeared on behalf of Mr Dickinson, and directed attention to the special rules, certified by the inspector, which had been violated. He said he had no doubt that Smith would feel as regrettable as any person that the explosion had taken place, as he was to some extent blameable. Smith pleaded guilty to not having the stopping plastered and to not appointing a fireman and said that the rule had been broken in not letting the air run through the pipes, but he pleaded not guilty to neglecting the ventilation. William Whittaker and Thomas Clegg gave similar evidence to that they gave at the inquest. Richard Hudson, colliery manager, said that he ordered a 6 inch pipe to be taken up, and a 12 inch pipe put in to keep up the ventilation through the chain drift. It was Smith's duty to see that the ventilation was kept up through the mine. Smith understood they were going to put up a stopping, and he went down purposely because of that. He gave orders to start Clegg's place 3 yards nearer the shaft. Mr Hudson said that on February 16th he gave the men lamps to go down, and gave the keys to the engineman every change of shift, so that no gas might come into contact with the naked light. No gas was seen on February 16th. Mr Hudson told Mr Grimshaw that mortar was always used for stoppings. Smith said the men were not blasting coal, but what was called white earth, and added that he forgot to put the mortar in, as there had not been any gas up to February 16th. He said he had learned his lesson for the future. Mr Grimshaw then asked Mr Dickinson if he wanted the full penalty to be imposed, but Mr Dickinson said no, as Smith seemed to have the confidence of his employers. He was therefore fined £1 in each case.

Accrington Times, November 28th 1874:- An accident happened on Tuesday at Baxenden Colliery to Richard Kenyon, a young man employed as an engine tenter at the pit bottom. The colliery workings have now extended so far that an endless chain, with an engine of some considerable power, extends half a mile to bring the wagons from the interior. Kenyon worked on this engine, and it seems that, if it is in a certain position when the chain is stopped, it needs needs a little help at the flywheel to get the crank over its centre. Kenyon, having turned the steam on, put his foot to the rim of the flywheel, when it suddenly revolved, and, before he could snatch it away, the next arm of the wheel caught it, smashing it horribly. The bones of the legs were also much bruised. He was taken home and Dr Connell attended him, successfully amputating his foot. Kenyon was a much respected workman, and great sympathy is expressed for him, as he is an orphan and the sole support for his sister.

The following article probably attracted little interest when it was published, but, over a century later, it gives us some fascinating details of Railway Pit.

Accrington Observer, June 12th 1880:- About 2.00 a.m. on Sunday a fire was discovered on the part of the works at Baxenden Colliery nearest the Lancashire and Yorkshire Railway. It was seen by several people at the same time, including the railway signalman, a young man coming from Accrington, and the son of Mr Parker who is employed at the works. By then the fire had got well hold of a wooden shed, beneath which were a set of coal screens and a small steam engine used for grinding the coal into slack for the coke ovens, a great many of which adjoin the building which was on fire. The coals are brought to the surface near Manchester Road and taken in tubs to the railway sidings by an elevated tramway. The screening boxes and machinery were fixed at the terminus of this tramway, and here the fire broke out. As there was a good deal of oil-saturated woodwork and a large quantity of coal and slack, the fire burned fiercely. The Accrington fire engine was sent for and in the meantime a hose pipe on the ground was got to play. Shortly afterwards the Baxenden Turkey Red Dyeing Co's fire engine arrived. The screens and the blacksmith's shop were connected by a wooden bridge, and the firemen's attention was directed to saving this part of the premises, which they did. The fire on the other part began to die out for want of combustible materials. The headgearing of an old pit shaft, connected with the screening shed, was partly destroyed. Accrington fire brigade was rather late in arriving, but the fire was soon got under control when 3 jets of water were turned upon the smouldering remains. Mr Whittaker, general manager, and a few of the underlookers were present the following morning. The damage is estimated at £600 and is not covered by insurance, as Messrs George Hargreaves and Co. have their own insurance fund.

Accrington Times, February 11th 1882:- *Yesterday Mr H.J. Robinson, coroner, held an inquest at the Derby Hotel on John Soddy, 40, labourer at Baxenden Colliery, who was found dead at the colliery the previous Wednesday. Mr Bolton, general manager of the collieries, Mr Arthur, and Mr Whittaker, sub managers, were present on behalf of the colliery company, and produced plans of the coal grinding apparatus used for making coke slack, explaining that, after the coal has been crushed, the slack is raised by elevators and emptied into a large iron box, from where it is drawn as required for burning in the coke ovens. The slack is carried into the box by mechanical appliances, and, as it is spread rather unevenly, the men go into the box to spread it out. The first witness, Mary Soddy, 15 St. James' Street, said her husband was quite well when he left for work on Wednesday morning and had worked at the colliery about 12 months. She told the coroner that he had once said he did not like going into the slack box, but did it because it was his duty. James Cockerill Kenyon, colliery labourer, said he saw Soddy go into the slack box with his shovel about 11.35. Mr Whittaker then stated that the box was about 16 feet by 12 feet, and would hold about 40 tons. There was a ladder inside. If Soddy was overcome by the dust, he had no way of raising the alarm. It was usual to empty the box while the men were inside. The hole at the bottom of the box was about a foot in diameter, and they could fill a wagon in a minute, keeping away from the hole when the box was being emptied. A person stepping on to the slack would only sink a few inches and could walk about the pan easily. Reuben Moore, Lydia Street, Accrington, said he worked at the coke ovens. On Wednesday noon he began to draw slack from the box in which Soddy was working and he saw him come through the hole. He raised the alarm, and he and several men went up the ladder and found Soddy was buried under the slack. It was 12.15 before they got the body out as there was 4 or 5 feet of slack on his head. Moore had just drawn a wagon of 15 or 16 cwt when Soddy's foot appeared, so he thought Soddy must have been right above the hole when he drew the hopper. Moore did not know that anyone was in the pan when he drew the hopper, but it was usual to give a warning when there was someone in. This could be heard inside the box even with the chain working and the mill going. Mr Bolton then said he thought that, at a previous drawing of slack, a cavity had formed in the pan and, as the drawing took place, Soddy had stepped on it and it had collapsed. Several jurymen thought that this must have been the case, as the drawing of 16 cwt of the full pan would not make much difference. George Barlow said the pan was filled twice a day, and it took one man an hour to spread the slack to make it hold more. He had been in the pan when the coal was drawn and could tread it down as fast as they could draw it. He once sank to the knees when they were drawing, but he had never found any hollow places in the slack and the men had never shouted to him when they began to draw as there was plenty of room to come out when the drawing began. Richard Whittaker, foreman, said he had been in the box when slack had been drawn and found no danger, adding that the slack was slightly damp. Mr Bolton said that in future they would not allow a man to go in to the pan and stand on the slack. The jury said that was satisfactory and returned a verdict of Accidental Death.*

RED DELPH PIT   NGR Unknown
This colliery was probably one of Mr Walsh's pits in the Dogshaw area of Over Darwen. Nothing else is known of it, but it was mentioned in the *Report on Child Labour* by Mr Austin, who compiled the following report.

William Holt, going on 19, works at the Red Delf Pit at Over Darwen. Gets coals, the seam of coal is about 20 inches, average, and the roof is cut away about a foot. He crawls up them on his hands and knees, and sits on a board and works the coals before him. They take their meals at work. They go to work in the morning. Have only one meal a day, never stops an hour to eat, only 20 minutes. Come away about six o'clock, some times five. When in full employment, works 10 hours piece work. Twelve tubs for 1s.10d, can do 12 in a day, but never in full work lately. There are about 15 altogether, most as young as him. He was a drawer since he was 6 years old. Thrutched first, and afterwards drew by the belt. Some thrutched with their head, because they cannot thrutch enough with their hands alone. Thrutching with their head makes a gathering in their head and makes them very ill, and yet the getters make them do it, and beat them if they do not. He had been beaten with pick haum, hammer and lumps of wood. It never made any bruises. Some gets their legs broke with being struck too hard. He has seen it when they have gotten an eye knocked out by whizzing stones at them. The work has been so slack that they cannot find clothes to go in. At Walsh's coal mine the water drips down the shaft, so that the hooker-on is always wet. He is a grown up person. The runs are dry except for underfoot. The children have flannel dresses to go down in, which are pulled off and put in a dry place near the eye of the pit, and they work nearly naked.

RED EARTH   SD718283
A drift mine worked by Shaw's Glazed Brick Co., Red Earth was situated in Yate and Pickup Bank near Darwen. It was mainly a fireclay works, though some coal was extracted from the Lower Mountain Mine. In 1960 the manager was Mr L. Aldritt, who oversaw 13 men below ground and 4 on the surface. This was William Henry Shaw's third drift mine and opened circa 1939. Its closure in 1963 marked the end of coal and fireclay extraction in the Darwen area. Remains include large areas of colliery spoil and various foundations.

Darwen News October 6th 1961:- Colleagues in the NUM have presented a cheque to their local secretary for 22 years, Mr Thomas Smith, 61, of 23 Worth Avenue. He is married with 2 sons and a daughter and has always taken a keen interest in the activities of the NUM. He is employed at Messrs Shaw's Glazed Brick Works who operate their own private colliery where Mr Smith is a surface worker. Mr Smith told us, "I've had a long and happy association as secretary of the NUM and have seen the movement grow from a very humble beginning." With the closing of the Hoddlesden Colliery, the Darwen branch is to be amalgamated with another branch in East Lancashire. Not so long ago, there were 120 members in the local branch, but following the competition from oil, a number of miners have left the industry. One of Mr Smith's last jobs as secretary was, with the co-operation of the NCB and Hoddlesden Colliery, to facilitate the transfer of NUM members to pits in the Burnley area.

PLATE XV Peter Wright Pickup (Gordon Hartley).

RISHTON COLLIERY   SD728300
The first sod was cut for Rishton Colliery shaft on November 7th 1883 and coal was reached a year later.

Blackburn Standard, November 29th 1884:- On Saturday a dinner was held at the Walmsley Arms, High Street, Rishton, to celebrate finding coal at the new colliery, Rishton, worked by Peter Wright Pickup. About 2 years ago the old mine, which was worked by the Dunkenhalgh Colliery Co., was worked out. Fourteen months ago workmen employed by P.W. Pickup began to sink a new shaft and on Thursday came across a good seam of coal.

Peter Wright Pickup was the son of Peter Pickup, who worked in partnership with Thomas Brooks in Brooks and Pickup, Towneley Collieries, Burnley. The pit was 525 feet deep and worked the Lower Mountain seam. It was at the top of Walmsley Street in the town, the dwelling there now having been the pit manager's house. The cobbled forecourt of the house was part of the paved yard of the pit. Gordon Hartley, of Burnley, while researching into the family history of, among others, Peter Wright Pickup, spoke with miners who had worked at Rishton pit. They told him they had to go about 2 miles to reach the coal face. The seam was about 18 inch to 32 inch and they used a sledge to get there. The coal was got out by picks and shovels and the miners bought these themselves from Gibson's ironmongers at the corner of Spring Street, Rishton. Directly under the war memorial in Rishton at 500 feet below ground is what was called West One, where 4 different haulage roads branched off.

The pit shafts at Rishton were filled in around August 1991, so that a road could be built for access to the South Side Estate. Water was pumped from the Rishton shaft to Rishton Paper Mill from around 1970 until 1983, when the latter closed. Just before Rishton Colliery closed in 1941, the underground workings broke into those of the old Whitebirk Colliery.

The 1938 *Colliery Year Book* names the colliery directors as P.W.P. Pickup of The Chestnuts, Fiskerton, near Nottingham, G.C. Pickup and G.T. Pickup. The secretary was F. Balmford, with J. Ward as chief engineer and F. Pelling as manager. There were 250 underground employees and 50 surface. The colliery worked the Lower Mountain seam and fireclay was also worked there. Electric power was used with 500 AC and 3300 AC voltage.

Accrington Times, March 15th 1884:- Mr H.J. Robinson, coroner, held an inquest at the infirmary on Friday on Edmund Ashton, 46, labourer, of 45 Fielden Street, Rishton, who died there on Wednesday. He was employed at Peter Wright Pickup's Rishton Colliery. On Tuesday February 26th, Ashton was helping to unload a winding drum, weighing about 4 tons, for the coal pit from a canal barge. The drum was raised on some packing about a foot high from the bottom of the boat, but the packing slipped, and the drum fractured his right leg so badly that it had to be amputated at Blackburn Infirmary, where he died a few days afterwards. A verdict of Accidental Death was returned.

Accrington Gazette, October 17th 1885:- About 9.45 on Tuesday a fatal accident occurred in Rishton coal pit, when Joseph Faramond, sinker, with about 10 other men was sinking a shaft at a depth of about 80 yards. A piece of wood weighing about 14 lbs fell from the top of the shaft and hit him on the shoulder. He was brought up the shaft immediately, and Dr Barr was soon in attendance, but he died about 15 minutes later without speaking. He was about 40 years old and leaves a widow and a large family. A native of Wigan, he lodged in Rishton. This appears to be a reference to the sinking of the second shaft at Rishton Colliery.

Accrington Gazette, April 4th 1894:- There was a fatal accident at Rishton Colliery at 14.30 on Tuesday, when a number of men were loosening props which supported the roof in a roadway. Among them was Jonathan Taylor, 26, fireman, of 2 Haworth Street, Rishton, who was dropping props by himself. When he had dropped about 6, a crack occurred in the lower part of the roof and, without notice, a long stone, about 5 feet thick and weighing about 10 tons, fell on him, crushing him almost beyond recognition. He was not got out till 3 hours later when he was quite dead. His body was then brought to the pit mouth, and taken home. He leaves a wife and a child. Mr H.J. Hargreaves held an inquest at the Walmesley Arms, Rishton, on Thursday. Also present were Mr Harrison, Inspector of Mines; Mr Reid for the Northern Accident Insurance Company; and Mr W. Pickup of Rishton Colliery. Richard Parker Banks, jig tenter at the colliery and of 2 Haworth

110

PLATE XVI Rishton Colliery.

Street, said Taylor, who had been a fireman for 4 or 5 years and had worked in the pit almost all his life, was his brother-in-law, and they lived together. Thomas Addison, 27 Edward Street, coal miner, said they had finished mining about 14.00 on Tuesday, and they then started to draw props. They had drawn 2 or 3, when Taylor, who was the manager of the men in that part of the pit, came up and began drawing props in another place. They cleared the place in case anything happened. Taylor used one of their hammers, and told one of them to shine the light in his direction so that he could belt the props out, as they would be there all night if they were not quick. He had belted 2 or 3 when he said the roof was nibbling down one side, and immediately the roof came in. Addison thought Taylor had drawn the props too hastily, as belting was not a proper way to get props out, even though he had sounded the roof with his hammer and said it sounded good before he started. They warned him about being careless and thought that, if he had worked quietly and slowly, he would have stood a better chance of getting out of the way. Another miner, Bolton, narrowly escaped being buried. Inspector Harrison said Taylor had been in too great a hurry. The Coroner agreed with this, saying there was no one else to blame. A verdict of Accidentally Killed was returned.

Accrington Gazette, September 14th 1912:- *Thomas Nolan, 17, drawer, of 14 Edward Street, Rishton, was killed by a rock fall while at work at Rishton Colliery on Monday. About 11.30 he went to collect some old timber on the east road in the mine when the roof and a large stone suddenly fell. Some men working close by heard the crash roof and at once went to the spot, but*

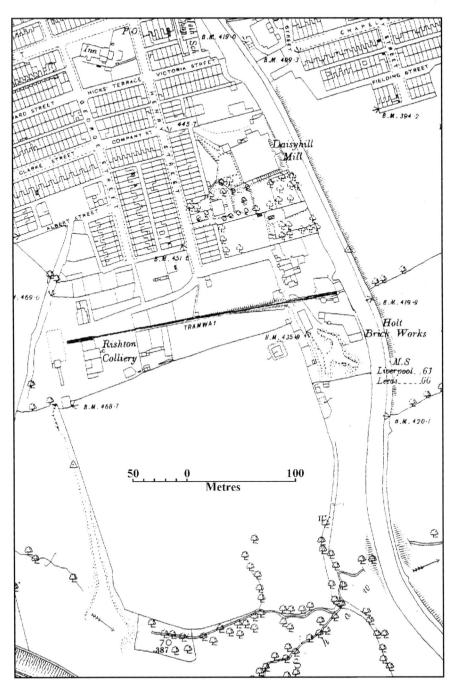

Fig. 22. *Rishton Colliery.*

Nolan was completely buried beneath the debris. He was got out in 30 minutes, but he had sustained a fractured skull and a fractured leg and was thought to have died instantly. Mr Halewood held an inquiry at Rishton Police Station on Tuesday, with Mr Rhodes, representing the colliery owners, and Mr G.B. Harrison, Inspector of Mines, present. Nolan's father said he was in good health when he left for work about 5.45 on Monday morning. Henry Dodd, collier, 20 Knowles Street, Rishton, corroborated the above and added that Nolan was taken to the bottom of the shaft where he was seen by Dr Salkeld, who pronounced him dead. James Rhodes, fireman, of 87 Haworth Street, said the place where the accident occurred was in a perfectly safe and satisfactory condition when he examined it about 5.30 in the morning. It was held up by props about 2 feet 5 inches apart and these had been all right when he examined them. He could not explain why the fall of earth had happened. A verdict of Accidental Death was returned.

Accrington Observer, December 4th 1925:- *John Whittle, 18, drawer, of 27 Cross Street, Oswaldtwistle, and Joseph Alfred Jones, 42, fireman, of 3 Suddall Cross, Blackburn, were killed at Rishton Colliery on Monday night. Mr D.N. Hazlewood, District Coroner, held an inquest with a jury at Rishton Police Station on Thursday. Mr H.A. Steele, Inspector of Mines, attended, as did Major A. Radcliffe Ellis of Wigan, representing the colliery proprietors, Messrs P.W. Pickup Ltd; Mr J. McGurk, JP, of the Miners' Federation; and Mr W. Miller of the Colliery and Fireman's Deputies' Association. Mary Whittle, 27 Cross Street, Oswaldtwistle, widow of Richard Whittle, general labourer, and mother of John Whittle, said that on Monday last her son went to work about 14.30 as usual. He had worked at Rishton Colliery about 4 years. James Ainsworth Cross Smith, of 13 Blackburn Road, Accrington, boot and shoe maker and brother-in-law of Joseph Alfred Jones, said Jones had worked at Rishton Pit for a number of years. He left home for work on Monday last about 13.45. John Bury, drawer, of 11 Whitebirk, said that about 18.45 he was working in the main chain road of No.1 West dip district, when Jones fired a shot in the roof. After doing so, Jones came and examined the place, and Whittle and Bury followed him. As they were returning, Jones remarked that the roof was bad. He was testing it when, without warning, a large stone weighing about 15 cwt. fell and pinned Jones and Whittle to the ground. Bury helped to remove the stone, and found that Jones and Whittle were dead. Their bodies were brought to the surface. He told Mr Steele that two shots were fired, at which time he was in a manhole up the chain road. The fireman, Jones, was round a corner about 30 yards away. He fired the shots and was examining the place, when, without his permission, Bury and Whittle went down with a tub, going one on either side. Bury was at the side away from the fall and it just caught his arm. Robert Nowell, assistant fireman, of 62 Church Street, Church, said that at 18.45 on Monday he was working with Jones who fired a shot, wrapped up the cable and afterwards examined the place. Shortly afterwards Nowell heard a crash and went to see what had happened. He raised the alarm and got assistance. He told Mr Steele that he was assisting Jones who was fireman in charge of the district and who had the authority to send the men out of the place if he found the roof was unsafe. Alexander Bray, deputy, of 40 Henry Street, said that on Monday he was in charge of No.1 West dip district. At 13.00 he examined the place where Jones and Whittle subsequently worked and found the roof quite safe, sound and secure. William Kehoe, colliery manager, of 29 Clifton Street, Rishton, said he was told of the accident at 20.40 on Monday, and immediately returned to the pit. The road where the accident occurred was 8 foot wide and 4 foot 6 inches high and Jones was working there to make the roof higher. A verdict of Accidental Death was returned.*

Blackburn Times, August 3rd 1929:- *Mr Maden, manager of Rishton Colliery, was fined £5, with costs of £8 11s 0d, for breach of the Coal Mining Regulations, following a fatality last January when Henry Neville Dobson was put to work to break through the coal to let some of the water from a flooded part of the pit. The place had not been worked for 3 months. Dobson worked there all Tuesday afternoon and came again on the Wednesday to work the same place, which was along a passage about 27 inches high and about 8 feet wide. At the end of the passage there were two other passages, one leading up and one leading down. The one leading down was about 8 yards from where Dobson was working in a sitting position. About 6.30 on Wednesday, Dobson was missing and the passage was found to be full of water. A pump working at a rate of 100 gallons a minute was immediately got to work, but it was not until 11.00 on Thursday morning that all the water was cleared. Dobson's body was found in the sump 35 yards from where he should have been working.*

Other deaths at Rishton Colliery include that of Hubert Hall, a local Methodist preacher who was a clerk at the colliery. In early June 1934 Mr Hall, for no apparent reason, threw himself down the shaft. His body was recovered from 9 feet of water in the sump. The inquest jury recorded a verdict of Suicide, with insufficient evidence to show the state of his mind.

Northern Daily Telegraph, Wednesday, September 14th 1955:- *A new road has been made opposite Phillips Road, Blackburn. The shaft at Blow Up Pit is covered in, and is about one yard from the new road and about 60 yards from the arterial road. The water in the pit is standing about 32 feet from the surface. The old colliery workings from Sett End, Whitebirk and Blow Up are all full of water, and water is still being pumped at Rishton Colliery to Dean Reservoir at Great Harwood for the Accrington and District Water Board.*

Accrington Observer, September 24th 1985 - '25 Years Ago':- *The NCB has asked Dunkenhalgh Estate for permission to demolish some of the buildings at Rishton Colliery which have been derelict since 1941. The NCB own the mine, but have to have permission of the Dunkenhalgh Estate as they own the land. Plans were afoot to install 2 new electric pumps at the mine, but before this could be done part of the mine's headgear had to be demolished. Since 1941 the mine has been used to pump water from a nearby lodge to Dean Reservoir which supplies Accrington and District.*

ROBIN FIELD NOOK   SD769268
This pit worked the Upper Mountain Seam and is marked on the 1848 OS Map as an old coal pit. Possibly short lived, it stood at the junction of Hollins Lane and Manchester Road, behind the Alma Inn at Baxenden, but there are no remains and the site is now used as playing fields.

ROTHWELL MILL   SD762268
Rothwell Mill pit is shown on a plan of 1784. It was 30 feet deep to the Lower Mountain Mine.

SCAITHCLIFFE COLLIERY   SD759283
There are no remains of this colliery, which was at the top of St. James' Street, Accrington, as the area has been completely landscaped. The first pit was sunk by George Hargreaves and Co. in 1859 to the Upper Mountain Mine at a depth of 180 feet. The seam was 30 inch thick on average, but the mine was abandoned in 1883. A second attempt was made to work the coal seams here during 1890-91, when two 540 foot deep shafts were sunk to the Lower Mountain Mine. Both shafts were brick lined throughout, and the seam averaged 26 inches in thickness. A wooden headgear was built over the upcast shaft, which was 10 feet in diameter. The headgear was 38 feet high, with backstays 60 feet long. Steel guide ropes, anchored at the bottom by cheese weights, were installed in this shaft which had two 6-man cages. The upcast shaft was 14 feet in diameter and had a single cage, wound by a small steam winder via a pulley built into the engine house brickwork. The Pillar and Stall method of mining was used in the early days of the pit and coal was hauled from the face in 4 cwt tubs by endless chain haulage whose main engine was situated at the shaft bottom. Drawers took the coal tubs to the main haulage for transportation to the shaft. Miners travelled to the coal face on sledges or trams, which were small 4-wheeled trolleys that ran on the rails. Squatting on his thigh on the tram, the miner propelled himself by pushing at each sleeper with one leg. He would have to travel long distances, often thousands of yards, before reaching his workplace. Going downhill on a tram was particularly hair-raising as the only method of braking was by forcing two wooden flaps fastened to the tram down onto the wheels. In later years, Siscol coal cutters were introduced. They undercut the headings and the coal was then broken by explosives. Electricity came to the mine workings on January 13th 1928, and was used to power a haulage from the No.2 Gearing on October 27th that year. On the surface, the old screens were dismantled in October 1927, and new ones brought into use on March 12th 1928. Rope driven haulage, over 1000 yards long, was introduced on a single track roadway from the shaft to the No.1 Gearing in late May 1929. In December that year, an Anderson Boyes coal cutter, with a 17 inch jib, was employed on the No.3 District. By 1930 power was

supplied by Accrington Corporation, and in 1932 the single tracked main haulage road was made double tracked. The majority of output from Scaithcliffe was delivered to Altham Coke Works, though a small amount went to the domestic market and local mills.[10] In the mid-1890s, Henry Smith was manager with 119 men underground and 16 on the surface. Workings at Scaithcliffe connected with several other collieries, including Broad Oak, Huncoat and Thorney Bank. Pithead baths were opened in 1937. The pit worked towards Accrington town centre, where pillars of coal were left to support buildings such as the town hall. Other workings progressed towards Accrington Victoria Hospital, Huncoat, and Moleside End. When it closed in 1962, Scaithcliffe Colliery employed 62 men underground and 14 on the surface. W. Oldroyd was the manager and S. Bollard the undermanager.

Accrington Times, July 4th 1874:- *Yesterday fortnight, Lawrence Walsh, a collier at Scaithcliffe new pit, met with a serious accident from his own carelessness. At present the drifts at the mine are few, and are not driven far. Gas is given off in moderate quantities, but there is excellent ventilation, which enabled Walsh to work with a naked light. He had unlocked his lamp with some simple instrument, but, when he went into another part of the mine, a seam was giving off gas freely. This fired on his light and burned his face, hands and arms severely. He is a married man with 3 children, and, his punishment having been so great, we understand that his employers do not intend to summon him for a breach of the regulations.*

Accrington Times, July 4th 1874:- *Mr Hargreaves, coroner, held an inquest on Monday at the Derby Hotel on Peter Griffiths, 15, who yesterday week was killed at Messrs George Hargreaves and Co's Scaithcliffe Pit. Mr Dickinson, Inspector of Mines, was present, and Mr Hudson, manager of the pit, submitted drawings of the workings. William Griffiths, collier, of Great Harwood, said the deceased was his son and was working as his drawer on the previous Friday morning when a roof fall occurred. Two stones fell from the roof, and one caught his son, who was about 3 yards away, on the head. The witness went for assistance to a man working 20 yards away, but, when they got the stone off, his son was dead. They had met with a fault and were cutting through it carefully. The witness had sounded the roof about 45 minutes before the accident and, as it did not sound bad, he had no fear of it. William Hughes, the gaffer, had also sounded it that morning. The cause of the fall was 2 slips meeting at the top of the roof. William Griffiths said he and his son had previously worked at the Dunkinfield [Dunkenhalgh?] Pit. He told Mr Dickinson that, although he knew that the slip was overhead, he had thought it too narrow to fall, being only a yard wide. There was no room to prop and there was no dribbling before the fall. Mr Hudson told the jury that the pit was 60 yards deep. Mr Dickinson said that it was not a good roof, and may not be called so in any part of the mine. Mr Hudson here said the slip was being cut through to improve the ventilation and clear away some gas. William Hughes,*

116

PLATE XVII Scaithcliffe Pit (Accrington Reference Library).

underground steward, said he had examined the roof about two and a half hours before the accident. It appeared to be safe, and he worked there about 20 minutes afterwards. Thomas Harrison, joiner, who laid Peter Griffiths out, said the spine, neck and right ankle were broken, and blood came from both ears and the mouth. The coroner said that this was an occurrence which took place quite suddenly, and which no presight could prevent. The father said he had been a collier for 30 years and had taken every precaution with a view to his son's safety and his own. The jury therefore could not do otherwise than return a verdict of Accidental Death.

Accrington Observer, January 4th 1947:- Included in the New Year's Honours list is Mr George Gorton, 66, of 1 Busk Meadow Street, Oswaldtwistle, who has been awarded the BEM for loyal and efficient service to the community as a mineworker. Mr Gorton entered the pit when he was 12 years old and, apart from 4 years in the Armed Forces in the 1914/18 War, has served all his working life in Messrs G. Hargreaves and Co's Scaithcliffe and Huncoat pits. Mr Gorton comes from a mining family, his father being one of the victims of the Moorfield Pit explosion disaster of 1883. A keen and active trade unionist, he has been associated with the NUM for over 50 years and is the present treasurer of the Accrington Branch. He is also a member of the Huncoat Pit Production Committee, which represents employees and employers, and is held in high esteem by his colleagues. An expert ambulance man, Mr Gorton has been a member of the pit ambulance brigade for many years. At one time a fireman, he was for a long period a coal getter, and, though he is not now engaged in that work, he is still employed underground. Mr Gorton has had 12 children, 9 of whom are still living. His wife died about 15 years ago.

Accrington Observer, May 25th 1954:- Built at a cost of £3,000, a new pithead bath at Scaithcliffe Colliery, Accrington, was officially opened on Saturday morning in the presence of representatives of the NW Division of the NCB Burnley Area. A neat compact building in brick on the pit bank, the bath has 9 shower points and will cater for nearly 200 workers. The opening was performed by Mr Reginald Lowe, area general manager, and Mr J. Whittaker, general manager of Accrington Collieries, presided. Among those present were Mr J. Duckworth, president of the NUM's Accrington Branch; Mr R. Bentley, divisional welfare officer; Mr E.E.D. Dawson Hall, Inspector of Mines; and Mr J. Bourne, divisional architect. There were also officials of NACODS and the Colliery Consultation and Baths Advisory Committee. Mr J. Whittaker announced apologies from Col. G.G.H. Bolton, divisional chairman of the NCB, and said that many there would remember his father opening the first baths in the Accrington Group at Calder in 1933. Others who apologised for absence were Mr Plover, Area Labour Director, and Mr Edwin Hall, secretary of the NUM's Lancashire Branch. Mr Whittaker said that the baths had been talked about for many years, but at first there was difficulty in finding a site. Once a site was found, however, the baths were speedily erected. Mr Whittaker added that a considerable amount of material and equipment for the new baths had been obtained from the original baths at Huncoat. Mr Whittaker then introduced Mr J. Duckworth as an Old Huncoater and one of the trusted and well loved employees of the old Accrington Collieries, to welcome those representatives present. In doing so, Mr Duckworth said he had been pressing for the last 8 years to get baths at Scaithcliffe, and added that they had been built in the very place he first suggested. The opener, Mr Lowe, was new to Accrington, having come with nationalisation. In that time he had been in charge of the Burnley area and had done all he could for the welfare of the employees. He went on to say that the workers there had never let him alone about the provision of baths, though the delay had been to some extent unavoidable as they had to consider the type of baths they could put up there. He added that their architect devised a type of baths suitable for small mines, and the one at Scaithcliffe was the best they could have. Mr Lowe concluded that the use of the baths was perhaps the greatest boon which could be given to the mine worker and said it was the NCB's intention to provide bathing accommodation for every mineworker in the area. After a tour of the baths, Mr J. Acornley, under-manager of Scaithcliffe Colliery, proposed a vote of thanks, seconded by Mr H. Whipp, president of the local branch of NACODS.

Accrington Observer, July 7th 1962:- Dick Shuttleworth, 64, gave a half hearted ring on the bell at Scaithcliffe Colliery, signalling that the last man had been brought to the surface. *Stained with coal dust, but wearing a smile, Albert Halliwell, 59, of 18 Accrington Road, Blackburn, walked out of the cage and joined his workmates for a brew. It was Friday June 29th when production stopped at the 100 year old colliery, which was statistically the safest in the north-west, and the third safest nationally, and the afternoon and night shifts joined forces for the last shift. The wheels will turn for a couple or more weeks, as equipment underground is transferred to other local pits, but no more 8-wheeled lorries will leave the yard loaded with coal. The colliery, which produced between 360 and 370 tons per week, has neared the end of its coal resources, after working continuously since 1850. Of the men who were employed at the pit, 61 will be found alternative employment. Albert Halliwell will always be remembered as the last man to leave the pit when production ceased. Stepping out of the small cage, he said, "I've seen everyone out, and left everything secure. I didn't like leaving it after being 45 years in the pit, and working here for 21 of those years. It was sad travelling those 180 yards from the bottom." The man who rang the last bell has now completed half a century in pits. Richard (Dick) Shuttleworth of 3 Hannah Street, Accrington, will carry on a few more weeks at Scaithcliffe, and then go into retirement.*

SCHOLES FOLD   SD696221

There was a coal pit near the Primitive Methodist Church and the railway line in the Hannah Street area of Darwen before Scholes Fold Colliery, but the latter was sunk by the Brandwood family around 1851. It worked the Yard Mine and caused serious subsidence in the area around Newbridge Mill and Redearth Road. The abandonment date of 1862, given by the *Catalogue of Abandoned Mines*, is contradicted by the following report.

Bacup and Rossendale News, March 12th 1864:- *John Adcroft, a miner at Scholes Fold Colliery, Over Darwen, was being hoisted out of the pit on Friday morning in a basket. Seeing he was about to be carried over the hoisting gear, he jumped out, but missed his mark, fell down the shaft and was dashed to pieces.*

SCOTLAND   SD718215

The site of this colliery is midway between Near Scotland and Far Scotland Farms, Blacksnape Village, and reached by a footpath from Chapman Road, Hoddlesden. Remains include an area of disturbed ground and colliery spoil. A number of workings are shown on the 1848 OS map, including a coal pit, an old coal pit, a coal drift and an old coal drift and two shafts sunk in search of coal. The mine was evidently abandoned by 1854, as it is not listed in Joseph Dickinson's *Statistics of the Collieries of Lancashire, Cheshire and North Wales*.

SHOREY BANK   SD692225

In 1862 C.E. and J. Potter sank 2 shafts to the Yard Mine, near Knott Mill in the Shorey Bank area of Darwen. Knott Mill was a paper works, dating from around the 1830s, and Darwen Technical School was built on its site. The Shorey Bank Colliery Co. worked the pit in 1869, with J.R. Whitehead as manager. It was abandoned in 1871 and nothing remains of it.

Blackburn Times, June 17th 1862:- Last week we recorded a serious accident at Messrs Potter and Co's new colliery at Knott Mills, in which three men were very badly injured. We must now record another accident at the same place at about 13.15 on Tuesday, when George Youd, Edward Bury, Robert Redmayne, Thomas Riley and John Ramsden were working at the bottom of the shaft, which is now some 65 yards deep. Ramsden and Youd had prepared a charge of about 2 lb. of blasting powder, and they were stemming it into the hole prepared for it. Whilst Redmayne and Riley were similarly employed, Bury was sending up tubs. Youd was holding the rammer, while Ramsden was striking with his hammer for him. When the rammer, as in the case of last week's accident, came into contact with the hard rock, it struck fire, igniting the fuse and exploding the shot, scattering large pieces on all sides. Youd was killed on the spot. Bury was badly bruised about the legs and chest, and Redmayne was severely injured. Riley and Ramsden were badly bruised and scorched. An alarm was at once given, and the other miners employed at the shaft bottom came speedily to the spot. The injured were immediately sent up the shaft in tubs and placed in the engine house. Youd was at once taken home and leaves a wife and 4 children. Dr Waith, his son and his assistant were on the spot and rendered all the assistance they could. Mr Whitehead, the manager, and D. Graham were also there. Mr J.G. Potter was promptly on the bank and burst into tears at the sad spectacle presented. The injured were then taken to their homes. Yesterday, the inquest was held at the Punch Bowl, Blacksnape, on George Youd, aged 37. The jury was made up of Joseph Place (foreman), John Hollis, William Pierce, Thomas Kenyon, Ralph Knowles, Joseph Eccles, John Duerden, William Cook, Joseph Bates, John Gregson, John Pickup and James Green. Thomas Riley of Blacksnape, sinker, said he had been at Shoreybank Colliery about 2 months and lately there had been 5 men to each 8-hour shift. George Youd had been employed about 5 weeks. At the time of the accident, Youd and Riley were drilling the white sand grit and they had got about 8 yards deep in the rock. They were about 50 yards from the surface. All the rock requires blasting and they use a steel drill. Youd had drilled a hole, and so had Riley. They borrowed each other's striker alternatively. They started drilling on Tuesday morning, at 2 holes about 5 feet apart and the other 3 men acted as strikers. Drilling stopped about 11.00. Youd's drill was about 33 inches deep, and Riley's was about 30 inches. About that time, Mr Whitehead and Mr Walsh, overlookers, came down to see that the work was done properly. They began to put the powder in at about 12.00, measuring it with the canister lid, which held about a gill. Riley put two tots into his drill hole, but Youd put two and a half in his. They then placed some dry clay into the holes and pressed it down with the hammer shafts. The fuse was put in and Youd rammed the powder down, so the fuse travelled to the bottom of the hole. It was usual to leave about 6 inches outside the drill hole. The powder would not explode until the fuse had reached the bottom of the hole. There would be about 40 inches of fuse in the drill hole. Youd had not rammed above 4 inches when the explosion took place and he was thrown down. Riley was pushed to one side, but not injured. An alarm bell was rung and Robert Entwistle, Walsh and another man answered it. Riley added that he had never known a blast to go off in the same way before, even though he had worked with powder for the last 22 years. He knew Youd and believed he had some experience in blasting. He told the jury he had not much experience with firedamp and thought the rammer might have struck fire against the rock, which was remarkably hard and fine, or the fuse might have been broken or damaged. Mr J.R. Whitehead, manager, said the cause of the accident was inexplicable to him. He believed that, with proper caution, the accident might have been avoided and, to prevent sparks being emitted from gritty or flinty stone in future, he had instructed that copper drills and copper stemmers should be used. He had received a letter from Mr Dickinson, Inspector of Mines, who knew of both explosions, advising the use of cartridges and dry sand. Robert Entwistle advanced a number of theories as to the cause of the accident, but did not feel inclined to blame anyone. Henry Walsh, foreman to Mr Jepson the contractor, stated that he had not given any positive instruction to the workmen, leaving every detail to their practical knowledge. The jury returned a verdict of Accidental Death.

SOUGH COLLIERY   SD701209

The site of this colliery, which was abandoned before 1854, can be found by going down Watery Lane, Darwen, to where a pair of new, semi-detached houses, called Clough, face older property on Clough Street. A footpath from here leads to allotments, where a triangular concrete column marks the capped shaft of Sough Pit. Little else is known of it, but possibly William Entwistle, who later worked the Rosehill Flag Pits, had some connection with it. Mike Rothwell relates that a water-driven whimsey was used to raise coal at the mine. In the 1840s, Sough colliery was worked by Mr P. Smalley.

Extract from the *Report on Child Labour in Coal-Mines 1841*:- *Mr P. Smalley, Entwistle, Sough Colliery, Over Darwen, parish of Blackburn. Children employed:- 1 at 7 years, 2 of 11. None can write, all can read, all attend Sunday school and public worship. They work from 9 to 10 hours daily, the wages average only 3 shillings paid by piece, the lowest earning 2s 6d, the highest 4 shillings per week. They are all drawers. Young persons:- 1 at 15 years, 2 at 17 years. Not one can write, all can read, and attend Sunday school and public worship. They are principally coal getters and earn 7s 9d a week on average, some getting as much as 12 shillings and some only 4s 6d per week. The mine is ventilated by openings communicating with another mine, and by shafts constructed for the purpose. The contractor states in his return that for 20 years past no accidents have occurred from any cause, not even a broken finger. There is no school or sick-fund connected with the works and, though every effort is made by the principal to put a stop to the utterance of bad language by the men and to punishment of the children, he has not been able to effectively put a stop to it. The drawers use a chain and girdle, and they are assisted by the younger ones as thrutchers, who become drawers when 11 or 12 years old. Only one adult is employed.*

SOUGH LANE COLLIERY   SD718261

This colliery, developed by Thomas Simpson and James Simpson Young in the 1840s, worked the Lower Mountain Mine and was linked with older workings at Bank Moor Pit (NGR SD722255). It seems to have been abandoned around 1860. The sough which gives its name to Sough Lane was a drainage adit, or tunnel, driven into the hillside for the pits in this area. Early 18th century bell pit workings can be seen up Sough Lane towards Belthorn, 3 or 4 fields back from the Sough Lane Ends Colliery, and to the rear of Sough Pits Farm. A terrace of cottages, known as Colliers Row, in School Lane was built in the early 1840s to house the miners at the nearby pits.

Two capped shafts, at the western end of Sough Lane at Four Lanes Ends, mark the colliery, but landscaping in 1978 removed all other traces. A tramroad from the colliery went under the road, via a tunnel, and ran NNW, along embankments, through cuttings and another tunnel, to a coal staithe at Knuzden Brook. Evidence suggests that horses or ponies were used to haul the tubs back to the pit top. There were also coke ovens at the coal staithe.

PLATE X Capped shaft at Sough Lane Pit (Jack Nadin).

122

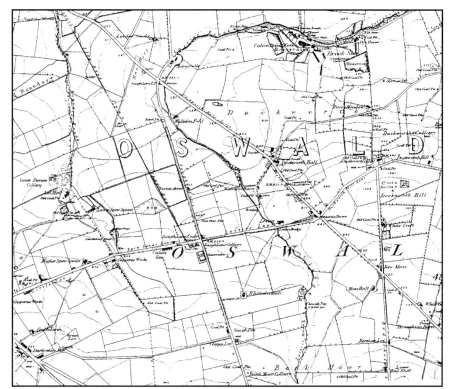

Fig.23 Sough Lane, Bank Moor and Low Darwen Collieries.

STANHILL COLLIERY   SD727274

Sunk around 1874 by Thomas Simpson and Co., Stanhill Colliery's workings were eventually merged with Aspen Colliery. This company still had the mine in 1896, when the *List of Mines* gave its address as 1 Rhyddings Street, Oswaldtwistle, Accrington. The coal, from the Lower Mountain Mine, was used for coking, heating and manufacture.

Darwen News, June 1st 1889:- *On Saturday morning, Richard Townley, collier, of Stanhill, was working getting pillars on the south-east side of Messrs Simpson and Co.'s Hot Hole coalpit at Lower Darwen, when loose earth and a 4 cwt stone fell on him, burying him so completely that only one leg was visible. Assistance was at once obtained, but his body was not recovered until life was extinct. At an inquest at Copy Nook Police Station on Monday, the jury returned a verdict of Accidental Death.*

TAG CLOUGH   SD771279

Marked on the 1893 OS map as a shaft, this was probably an air pit, or manriding shaft, for the Broad Oak and Cat Hole Drifts. The drift at the former is in a direct line with Tag Clough Shaft, which has been landscaped.

123

A possible site of the shaft is at the base of the gnarled tree where there is a water-filled hollow and a couple of large steel tanks.

TAYLOR'S GREEN   SD707214

This location had a long tradition of coal mining, and Hattons Colliery worked here in the 1840s. Taylor's Green Pit, locally called Clink Pit, dates from the early 1870s, with a fireclay works being added soon after. It was also called Thomas Knowles' Spring Vale Fireclay Works. In addition to fireclay, coal was extracted from the Little, the Ten Inch, and the Half Yard Mines. Richard E. Knowles, possibly related to the owner, was manager in the 1890s, when there were 27 miners and 3 surface men. Mining ceased in the Ten Inch (Lower Foot) in 1929, according to the *Catalogue of Abandoned Mines*, but continued in the Lower Foot and Half Yard until 1943. No more coal was mined, but fireclay was extracted until the mid-1950s.

The site was off Roman Road, north-west of Blacksnape, and can be reached from Blacksnape village, via a footpath below the Red Lion public house. Playing Fields Cottage was the site of the Punch Bowl Inn, which is mentioned in a number of inquests. Bearing left, follow the wall through the playing fields to emerge into an area of disturbed ground. This is part of the Taylor's Green site, much of which appears to have been incorporated into the housing development at Spring Meadow.

Besides mining coal, the firm made a number of sanitary fittings, pig and horse troughs, chimney pots, etc, and an elderly Blacksnape resident told the writer that Thomas Knowles was the inventor of the water trap, or U bend, locally called the Darren bend and also listed as such in the catalogues of builders' merchants. The ceramic side of the business continued by purchasing the necessary raw materials until 1970. The site was then used for a time as a storage area for North Western Ceramics, and later for Hepworth's Pipes. The 4 mine shafts at Taylor's Green Colliery appear to have been filled, but large areas of spoil and broken pipes still litter the place at the time of writing.

Blackburn Times, February 15th 1876:- *On Tuesday morning there was a fatal explosion of gas at Spring Vale Colliery. About 6.15, Anthony Cottom, of 29 Carr Row, Darwen, and Thomas Walsh, both firemen, descended the shaft to see if all was right in the mine. At the shaft bottom, they separated, each taking opposite directions. Cottom had with him a lighted lamp and a candle, but the latter was not lit. Walsh returned up the shaft, but Cottom did not do so, and a search was made for him. The manager (John Jepson) and his brother (Ralph Jepson) took a lighted lamp and, when opening a door about 200 yards up the mine, the stench of gas was so strong that they had to retreat. In a short time they were able to proceed with their search and found Cottom lying on his back. He was badly burnt all over, his skull was fractured, his arms broken, and he had others injuries. Yesterday, Mr Hargreaves, coroner, held an inquest on him at the Bridge Inn, Spring Vale.*

Betsy Ann Cottom, his widow, said he left home about 3.30 on Tuesday morning and did not return. James Walsh, of Borough Lane, fireman, said that he and Cottom went down the pit about 6.00 on Tuesday morning, each with a lamp to examine the pit. About 10 minutes after their arrival at the bottom, Walsh heard an explosion. There were no men working there at the time, but about 18 men were employed at the works. He told Mr Dickinson, Inspector of Mines, that both lamps were lighted in the cabin, but were not locked. He added that he last saw Cottom at the shaft bottom and 10 minutes afterwards he heard an explosion, the blast from which blew his own lamp out. Walsh then confirmed that he and Cottom had worked at the colliery for about a month and that the manager John Jepson had appointed him (Walsh) as assistant fireman. Jepson had also instructed him how to test for firedamp by having a little light in his lamp and holding it at the top of the mine, but had not told him about having the lamp locked. Cottom's lamp was found near his body and appeared to have been burnt. John Jepson, of 6 Grimshaw Street, Over Darwen, spoke next, confirming that he had been manager of the pit for 6 weeks. He said he had told Cottom and Walsh to be careful, but there had been no explosions at the pit before and the miners worked with naked candles. He could not give a reason for the explosion, unless it was a change in the weather. Mr Dickinson suggested that the water could have reached the roof of the tunnel and cut off all ventilation from the pit, as it had been closed from Saturday until Tuesday morning. Jepson agreed that this was possible. He said that when he appointed Cottom and Walsh he did not ask where they got their knowledge of gas from and gave them no instructions other than to be cautious when they were doing

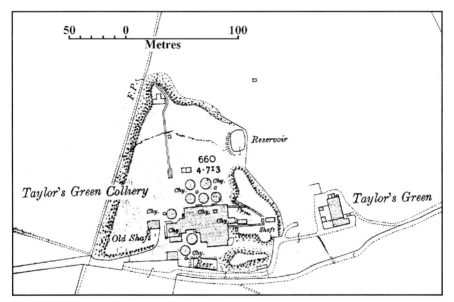

Fig.24 Taylor's Green Colliery.

their rounds. John Kay, watchman, said he had laid out the body. William Taylor, a director and former manager of the company, said that he had objected to John Jepson being appointed manager as he did not think his intelligence was sufficient for the job. He was not satisfied with him or with his way of carrying on the works. He (Taylor) thought Cottom and Walsh were incapable of performing the duties imposed upon them as they were both too young and had had no experience of gas before. He thought Jepson also had no experience of gas, but he did not know much about him other than he had worked a little at a colliery as manager. Taylor then said he never knew any gas to accumulate before the last step was cut, and added that the manager was responsible for the system of ventilation, which at that pit was by air pipes which were inadequate to work properly. The Coroner then reminded the jury that the inquest was to find out who was responsible for Cottom's death and added that, if Cottom undertook to do the work, he really was responsible, even though he might have been wrongly appointed to the job, as he knew he was incapable of it. They had to find out if anyone was criminally responsible for Cottom's death. As to past management, and the future management, Mr Dickinson would see to that. The Coroner thought Cottom was responsible for his own death, but Mr Dickinson said there was more responsibility than that as capable men should be appointed. He thought the matter should be further gone into and questioned the director further. The director said there would not have been an explosion, but for the ventilation, which he believed had stopped as there was a great deal of water in the tunnel. He thought the manager was to blame for Cottom's death through ignorance as he could not write and was not a certified manager. Taylor also thought Jepson was incompetent and had no experience of firedamp. The room was then cleared for the jury, who came to a verdict of Accidental Death. The Coroner told them that they could make a representation to Taylor, as one of the directors, if they thought proper and the jury decided this should be done. William Taylor was recalled and told that the jury wished him to convey to all the directors that they should be more careful in their appointments. He agreed to do this. John Jepson was recalled and told by the Coroner that, in taking the appointment of manager, he was taking a great responsibility. He was the responsible party to appoint everyone connected with the works, and a competent fireman was most essential. If he could not be depended upon, there was no safety in the pit. The jury thought he (Jepson) was scarcely fit to discharge the duties he had undertaken. Now, if he was not, he must think whether it would not be his duty to be relieved from office rather than run the risk of danger. He had the whole management of the pit and appointed his own firemen, and therefore was responsible, and if anything serious occurred he would be the first person answerable. The Coroner told him to consider that, and Jepson replied that he felt confident that he was capable of managing the works, having worked a colliery all his life. However, the foreman of the jury commented, 'If I was Mr Jepson, I would give up the situation'.

PLATE XIX
Thomas Knowles Ltd, Spring Vale Works and Taylor's Green Pit
(Darwen Reference Library).

Darwen News, May 18th 1898:- *An accident occurred at 10.45 on Monday morning at Messrs Thomas Knowles and Co's Colliery, resulting in the death of one man and the serious injury to another. At the time, 4 men were engaged about the pit. Two were getting coal, one was at the pit bottom drawing coals out, whilst the other, also a drawer, was at the pit mouth. The dead man was Edward Riley, 30, married with 3 children, the eldest just over 3 years old. The injured man is William Henry Baron, 43, also married and of 11 Bury Fold Lane. Riley was working a few yards further in the pit than Baron, getting coal from a point forbidden by the manager. This coal was comparatively easy to get, but it is known among the men that it is dangerous to work it. Baron, whose job was to take soundings of the roof, had just done so when the accident took place. He had assured himself that all was right, when, without a moment's warning, the roof caved in, bringing down about 100 tons of earth, stone and coal. George Egan, the drawer, was luckily just outside this particular workings, and escaped without injury, but Baron, who was just within, was pinned to the ground by an immense stone. Riley, however, had no chance of escape and was crushed and buried alive. Egan rushed to Baron's assistance, but he found it impossible to remove the stone without help. He communicated with those above, and when Baron was at last extricated it was found that his left thigh had been broken 6 inches above the knee. He was brought to the surface and taken to East Lancashire Infirmary, where he is now making fair progress. The men having extricated Baron, redoubled their efforts in search of Riley. Shortly after Monday midnight one of his arms was found, and*

127

about 2.30 on Tuesday morning his body was recovered. His position indicated that he had made a desperate attempt to escape. Pending an examination of the workings by the Mines Inspector, the pit is closed.

TITHE BARN   SD701231
Tithebarn, sometimes known as Dandy Row Colliery, was originally worked by the Brandwood family from the mid 1850s, taking coal from the Yard Mine. There was a temporary closure circa 1860. A decade later the colliery was reopened by the Eccleshill Coal Co., but was abandoned in 1882. It was situated near the junction of Pothouse Lane and the Roman Road, but no remains are evident as the site has been built over.

Accrington Times, August 14th 1875:- Hugh Stanton, 12, drawer and stepson of Thomas Halliwell, labourer, of 2 Bury Court, Chapels, died in Blackburn Infirmary on Saturday. In February last, he was at work in No.2 Tithebarn coal pit, belonging to the Eccleshill Coal Co., when he was struck by something falling from the cage and his skull was fractured.

TOP O'TH' COALPITS   SD687264
This was an old coal pit located on what was then called Coal Pit Moor, to the east of Ewood, between Darwen and Blackburn. The 1844 OS Map shows no fewer than 6 old coal pits in close proximity. According to Gordon Hartley, "*Around 1720, one John Bailey started to build a farm, to be named Coal Pit Farm on Coal Pit Moor.*".[11] Hartley also tells us:-

Blackburn Corporation hospital (Park Lee) was built in 1894 on land near to Coal Pit Farm. Circa 1935, 2 quarrymen descended a number of shafts near to the farm. The shafts were said to be around 50 feet deep and about 4 feet wide. At the base of one of the shafts they were able to crawl along the tunnels where the coal had been taken out, the seams varied from 2 feet 3 inch to 4 foot. The galleries run a distance of about 50 feet towards and under the hospital grounds. When the new quarry was opened around 1900 by Messrs Whitaker on Coal Pit Moor, fireclay was also worked at a depth of 50 feet beneath the coal seam. Rubble from the old Blackburn Market was used to fill the quarry in the late 1960s, early 70s.[11]

The coal pit, along with other parts of the estate, was advertised for sale in 1796.

Blackburn Newspaper, May 11th 1796:- The Property of Mr Bailey. The fee simple and inheritance of the estate commonly known by the name of Coal Pits, within the townships of Lower Darwen and adjoining the Township of Blackburn, now in the possession of Henry Barton and others, consisting of an ancient and respectable stone mansion or dwelling house, four cottages, a barn, stables, shippon and other outbuildings and about 40 acres of land. On this estate is a valuable coal mine, now in use, which makes from £60 to £70 per annum clear. Also a factory used for carding and spinning cotton and wool by means of a horse gin.

Fig.25 Horse Gin at Top o'th' Coal Pits, Blackburn.

In January 1846, Charles Haworth made a rudimentary sketch of Top O'Th'
Coalpits, which had by then been abandoned, see fig. 25.

TOWN BENT   SD739265

Thomas Simpson and Co. began sinking this colliery in 1889 and found the
Top Bed or Upper Mountain Mine at a depth of 18 yards. The seam was 26
inches thick. The Lower Mountain was cut at a depth of 97 yards and was
20 inches thick.[12] During the mid 1890s, Town Bent Colliery employed 181
miners underground and 21 men on the surface and was managed by Joseph
Thompson. There was also a drift entrance to the workings and, when Aspen
Colliery flooded in April 1909, its miners used it to get to safety. In March
1907, Oswaldtwistle Council's fire engine attended when several of the
wooden sheds on the pit-top were alight. The estimated cost of the damage
was £500, but none of the colliery's engines, boilers or shafts were affected.
A photo in Accrington reference library shows a group of the Town Bent
Colliery Rescue Team wearing breathing apparatus and clogs and carrying
safety lamps.

Today the site is best approached from Roe Greave Road, Oswaldtwistle.
Just before the Rhoden Road terrace of houses, turn down a rough track on
the left. The colliery was in the field in front of Town Bent Bungalow. The
local farmer told me that it was not very big and *was more like a shanty
town with wooden buildings.* The workings were so shallow that his father

129

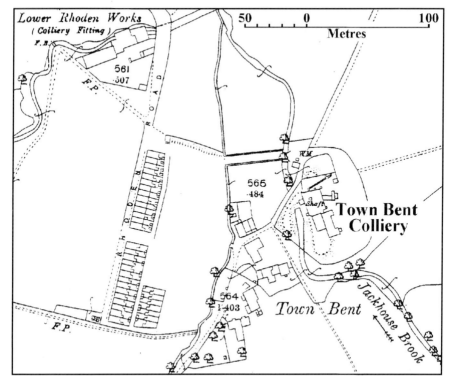

Fig.26 Town Bent Colliery.

could hear the miners working! When the site was being landscaped, he could look down into the pit and see the underground galleries. Hollows still appear on his land where the workings are subsiding. Town Bent Farm was owned by John Charney and his family for many years.

Accrington Observer, May 2nd 1890:- *On Saturday the sinkers and employees at the new Town Bent Colliery sat down for a supper at the Golden Cross, given by Messrs T. Simpson and Co. to commemorate the completion of sinking the pit. About 35 sat down for the supper.*

Accrington Gazette, April 15th 1893:- *Patrick Dooley, labourer, 50 and married, of 6 Back-house Street, off Union Road, Oswaldtwistle, was killed at Mr Thomas Simpson's Townbent coal pit on Wednesday. He looked after an endless chain, to which was attached buckets of slack coal which were emptied down a chute. About noon, Joseph Hartley, a labourer, took a tub to the chute to get it filled with slack coal. Before putting it under the end of the chute, he shouted to Dooley at the top to look out. When Dooley replied, "All right", Hartley pushed the tub under the chute, which opened a spring door to let the coal down. When he got the tub filled, he was levelling the coal with his hand when he saw Dooley's legs protruding*

130

through the bottom of the chute with his head up. The engine was quickly stopped, but meanwhile the coal had continued to enter the chute, with the result that Dooley was suffocated. Assistance was procured, and he was extricated in about 10 minutes. Dr Townley was sent for, but Dooley was dead. The inquest returned a verdict of Accidental Death.

Accrington Advertiser, July 20th 1900:- *About 10.30 a.m. on Wednesday, Richard Brindle, collier, 55 and married, of 369 Union Road, Oswaldtwistle, was killed while working at Oswaldtwistle Colliery Co.'s Town Bent Pit. He and Henry Hayes were filling a wagon, when some props used in the workings gave forth a cracking noise. Hayes shouted to his mate, "It's coming, Dick!" and both set off at a run. Brindle was, however, too late to save himself, and a portion of the roof came in on top of him, crushing him terribly about the head. Hayes escaped with a slight back injury. The inquest will be held today.*

Accrington Observer, June 30th 1903:- *"Thomas Walmsley, 27 and married, of Whins, Oswaldtwistle, was killed on Friday at Town Bent Colliery. He was working with Jeremiah Sullivan, of 8 Victoria Street, and William Walmsley, of Higher Twinch, when a stone weighing 12 cwt. fell upon him from the roof, killing him instantly. The stone had to be broken before his body could be removed. Mr Robinson, coroner, held an inquest with a jury yesterday at the Black Dog Inn, Oswaldtwistle. Mr Gerrard, Mines Inspector, and Mr Haworth, managing director of Oswaldtwistle Collieries, were also present. Sarah Ellen Walmsley, widow of Thomas, said she last saw him alive at 6.00 a.m. on Friday. He had worked all his life in coal mining, but that week he had worked on Wednesday and Thursday, but not on Tuesday. Francis Ince, fireman, of 4 Back Rhoden Street, Oswaldtwistle, said he examined the place in which Walmsley worked about 5.45 a.m. on Friday. He tried the roof and it was then quite safe. He told Mr Gerrard that he saw there was a step seam, or weakness, in the roof and he sounded near to that very carefully. He thought it was safe for anyone to go under. He saw Walmsley under the stone and thought he was under about the middle* [of the step seam]. *A colliery rule fixed the distance of props at 2 feet 6 inches, finished at night. In the morning when work started, however, they were rather more and also when the accident happened. Mr Gerrard suggested that, as Walmsley hewed away the coal, he gradually took away the support of the stone and it dropped without any warning. Ince agreed and also agreed that he would not expect a stone like that to give any warning, being free on all its sides. Mr Gerrard then pointed out a number of places in the vicinity of the accident where the props exceeded the fixed distance, and told the witness that these distances did not correspond with the rule. Pointing to where the accident happened, the witness replied that Walmsley had gotten that nook off during the morning. Ince was not there when Walmsley started work, but he thought it was at 7.00. The accident happened at 7.45. Ince agreed that in 45 minutes they would not get such a lot of coal and admitted that he just guessed the distance of the props and did not*

PLATE XX Town Bent Colliery (Accrington Reference Library).

measure them. Mr Gerrard pointed out that the rule for fixing props and distances was put into force as a result of fatalities caused by roof falls and that, if it was to be of any use, it must be carried out and the distances insisted upon. He then said that the rule had not been carried out in this place, the distances were too great and that was one of the reasons this accident occurred, especially as there were 3 weaknesses in this roof. Ince said he forgot to warn Walmsley about the step seam and Mr Gerrard said that, as a fireman and official appointed to do all that could be done to prevent such sad fatalities, he (Ince) might have done more than he did. Ince said that in future he would be more careful and would draw the workmen's attention to the roof and do all he could to carry out the timbering rules as to the distance of the props. Mr Gerrard continued by saying that it was no use posting notices that supports must only be 3 ft. 2in. apart, then letting them be set at 4ft. Jeremiah Sullivan, 40, of 8 Victoria Street, said he had worked with Walmsley on Friday morning. Walmsley was getting coal at the time of the accident and Sullivan was about a yard from him when the stone fell. He told Mr Gerrard that he knew the rule about the props and thought the distance where they were working would be about 27 to 30 inches when they started. He agreed that one prop put up would have saved Walmsley's life, but said they were not aware at that time. He had not worked on Thursday or Wednesday and Mr Gerrard pointed out that irregularity in working led to mistakes like this. Sullivan said that, even if he had been working, he might not have known about the step seam. The fireman had not told him about it and he did not know that the fireman knew about it on Wednesday night. If he had known that not only the step seam was there, but also another slip running at right angles, making it still weaker at the other end, he would have said that there should have been a prop put under it. Pointing to the diagrams, Mr Gerrard indicated a spot where the props on the Wednesday and Thursday had been much closer, whilst at the step they were further apart. He told Sullivan that he only wanted to encourage him to take more care and above all to remember that, when there was a rule which said that props should not be more than 27 or 31 inches apart, it should be taken notice of. Sullivan said he had always tried his best and did not generally go above 4 feet. He added that props of the right length had been available for use. The coroner remarked that accidents were often due to want of care on the part of the miners themselves. The men liked as much room as they could get, and preferred to have more elbow room and run a risk. A verdict of Accidental Death was recorded.

Accrington Observer, March 12th 1906:- Following an accident at Town Bent Pit, Oswaldtwistle, on Saturday evening, George Scholes, 15, son of Thomas Scholes, the mine manager, of 365 Blackburn Road, Oswaltwistle, is in the Victoria Hospital, Accrington, in a critical condition. Scholes, a joiner employed at Lower Rhoden, visited the mine to see what progress was being made in repairing the damage done by the fire the previous Wednesday. The buildings at the pit head are in 2 storeys, and whilst going round, Scholes fell from the higher storey to the lower, a distance of about 15 feet. He landed on his head on the edge of an iron coal-crushing machine, fracturing his skull. He was picked up unconscious. He was attended by Dr Townley, and removed to the Victoria Hospital. On Sunday he had not regained consciousness, and yesterday he had frequent relapses into an insensible condition.

TWO GATES   SD701226
Around 1855, John Brandwood sank a 108 yard shaft to the Half Yard Mine in the Ellison Fold area of Darwen. The Eccleshill Coal Co. worked the pit in the 1870s, but it had closed by 1880. The site is reached by a footpath behind Two Gates Mills, Anyon Street, near Two Gates Drive. Two large spoil heaps are visible. The one nearer the mill was the site of No.2 Pit.

Blackburn Times, March 9th 1861:- Richard Lightbrown, 13, son of John Lightbrown of Ellison Fold, died after an accident at Two Gates Colliery last Friday. Employed by the Exors of the late John Brandwood, he was ascending the pit in a basket at 16.00 on Friday when one of the chains became unhooked from the basket and he fell 108 yards to the shaft bottom. When taken up he was not quite dead, but expired about 19.30. An inquest held the Albion Inn recorded a verdict of Accidental Death.

VICTORIA PIT   SD763262

Also known as Friar Hill Pit, this mine at Baxenden worked the coal under Bedlam, Friar Hill and Accrington Moor. George Hargreaves and Co. sank the shaft circa 1855, probably as an extension to the Railway Pit workings in the valley below. It was around 330 feet deep to the Lower Mountain Mine. The Upper Mountain Mine was worked for a while in connection with Miller Fold and Dewhurst Collieries. Victoria Pit had passed to Hargreaves Ashworth Co. in 1869, and was abandoned in 1894. A ginney, running through the fields, linked it to Baxenden Colliery.

The site of the pit can be found by going down the lane to Green Haworth golf course, bearing left at the junction beyond the club house to Victoria Cottages on the left. In conversation with the present occupier of Victoria Cottages, it emerged that the person who filled or capped the shaft at Victoria Pit was given the cottages as a reward for his efforts. To the left of the cottages is the reed-filled reservoir of the pit, and, at the far end of the garden, are some large stone engine beds. The cottages were originally two dwellings and, in the 1870s, Henry Coupe, 52, banksman, lived in one with his wife, Elizabeth, and Elizabeth Bennett, with her sons, James, 19, coal miner, Henry, 13, and Edwin, 11, drawers in the mine, lived in the other.

Accrington Times, June 29th 1867:- Mr J. Dean, deputy coroner, held an inquest on Thursday into the death of John Mills, 17, drawer at Friar Hill Colliery, New Accrington. Mr Bolton, manager for Messrs Hargreaves, Ashworth and Co., was present. The first witness was Mr John Mills, of Wood Nook, Accrington, father of the deceased, who said his son left home for work last Monday morning and he was brought home dead that same morning. Henry Butterworth, collier, of Green Howarth, Oswaldtwistle, said he worked at the same pit as Mills and, at about 7.15 a.m. on Monday, he, Mills and several others were waiting to go down the shaft. Mills was

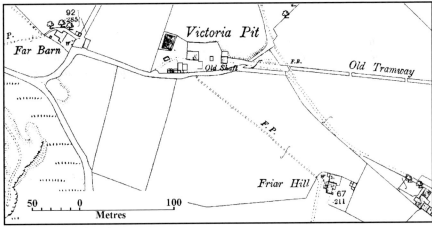

Fig.27 Victoria Pit.

standing about a foot from the pit mouth and his head fell to one side, and then the other, and then he fell down the shaft. Butterworth concluded that Mills was having some kind of a fit. The pit was 110 feet deep, and Mills fell to the bottom of it. The pit mouth was usually fenced round with iron railings, but at the time of the accident one side of the rails had been removed for repair. It was from that side that Mills fell. The rails had been there on Sunday morning. George Avery, 12, son of George Avery, of Baxenden, pit manager, said he was at the pit top last Monday. He knew John Mills and saw him standing near the pit mouth, with one hand on the conductor. His head fell a little backwards, and then he fell down the pit. He did not try to catch hold of anything as he was going down. His eyes were closed when he fell, and his hands were by his side. Avery added that he could not tell if his face was altered, as it was always white. He told a juror that Mills was about 2 feet from the pit mouth at the time he [Avery] was there. John Nuttall, collier, of Victoria Street, Anthony, said he did not see Mills fall down the pit, but assisted in removing him from the shaft bottom. He believed the body fell against an iron bar that was across the cage which was coming up, as the bar was bent. Mills was much injured on the head, his left arm was broken above the elbow, his left thigh was broken and there were several other injuries to his body. The rails were round the pit mouth on Saturday, and on Monday morning one side was absent, but it was not dangerous being in that state, as anyone could see it. He told Mr Bolton it was not dark, being about 6.00 a.m. at the time. Nuttall added that he had worked there for the last 5 years and the side gates were not up 12 months ago. At the part where Mills fell, the railings had not been up for more than 4 months. George Smith, underlooker, said that he did not see the accident occur, but the shaft had been fenced off about 3 months. He had worked at the pit 7 or 8 years. On Saturday morning one side of the railings was removed, leaving that side of the shaft where Mills fell unprotected. He told Mr Bolton that there would have been no difficulty in a person seeing that the railing there was removed, and told a juror that none had fallen down before. The fence had been put up because on dark winter mornings it was dangerous, as the mouth of the shaft could not then be well distinguished. The coroner in summing up remarked that it was highly desirable that the mouth of the shaft should be protected, but the law did not make it obligatory upon colliery owners to do so, and he was glad the precautions had been taken by Mr Bolton, the manager. The jury could not incriminate anyone, and he thought the verdict should be one of accidental death. He thought it probable from the description of Mills' appearance before he fell that he might have been dead before he fell down. A verdict of Accidental Death was returned.

The following two reports are on an accident that killed an 8 year old boy, who worked underground at Victoria Pit almost 30 years after the passing of the 1842 Coal Mines Act. The £5 fine imposed on the underlooker who employed the child reflects what little value was placed on children's lives at that time.

Accrington Times, November 19th 1870:- *Mr Hargreaves, coroner, held an inquest on Tuesday at the Bay Horse Inn, Baxenden, on James Barnes, 8, who was killed in Messrs G. Hargreaves and Co's Victoria Pit on November 9th. Mr Duckworth, Government Sub-inspector, was present at the enquiry. John Smith of Baxenden, ginney tenter, said that last Friday about noon he was putting a load on a wagon. Barnes at that time had left off work and was going along the chain road. Smith saw him underneath one of the wagons, which was full of coal. Barnes lay across the rails with his head underneath. Before Smith saw him, he thought something was wrong and gave the signal to stop the chain. He sent for assistance and James Rishton came. Smith did not see how Barnes was caught by the wagons, as he was 100 yards away, but he saw him go down the chain road. Barnes had a lighted candle with him and was walking between the rails. The chain road was about 4 feet wide, with about 2 feet clear of the passing tubs, and the travelling road, which Smith had told him to use, was between 2 and 3 feet. James Rishton, miner, said James Smith sent for him and, when he got there, he found Barnes laid dead under a wagon which appeared to have dragged a short distance. Barnes generally worked from 6.00 a.m. to 4.00 p.m., and attended school two half days a week. His job was to run empty wagons from the chain to be taken by the drawers to the colliers. The place is about 400 yards from the pit bottom, and the chain goes some distance further. There is no stopping place there, but there is a pulley to keep the chain up so that the trams were loosened. Those that are to go straight forward are pushed along without stopping, and those that are wanted for the colliers, he takes off the chain. His candle was out. He may have been running back, and been caught by the chain and knocked under the full wagons. James Barnes, Friar Hill, said the deceased was his son and he was 8 the previous March. He went to school a day in the week. His father did not know it was contrary to the Act of Parliament at his age to be thus employed, as he was not a drawer, but a runner of empty wagons. The father had been lamed on his back and had been out of work 18 months. Robert Geldard, underlooker, employed the boy out of pity. His father did not tell him his age, and did not know whether the underlooker inquired. Barnes told the inspector that he had 6 children when James was alive, the eldest being 12. Robert Geldard, underlooker, of Alliance Street, told the coroner that, when the boy's name was given, he was nearly 9 years, and he was employed at the latter end of July. The inspector explained that the law required that no boys should be employed who were less than 9 years old. The boys employed were required to attend school two half days in a week, and each attendance to be not less than 3 hours long. The coroner summed up the evidence, and remarked that the violation of the Act of Parliament was a matter for the consideration of Mr Dickinson. The jury returned a verdict of Accidental Death.*

Bacup Times, December 31st 1870:- *At Accrington Police Courts on Thursday, Robert Geldard, underlooker for Messrs George Hargreaves and Co's pits at Baxenden, was fined £5 and costs for employing a boy under the age of 10 years underground in November last. The lad had been killed in the pit on 9th November, being run over by a wagon.*

Accrington Times, February 3rd 1872:- *Last Tuesday night, Rufus Riley, 34, collier, of Bedlam, died from injuries received the previous Thursday at Messrs George Hargreaves and Co's Friar Hill coal-pit, Bedlam. At the time he was removing a pillar, when a quantity of roof fell and caught him. He was got out by his fellow workmen, but had sustained a fracture of the skull, a fractured left leg and other injuries. Medical assistance was immediately obtained, but he died from his injuries. A widower, Riley leaves 5 or 6 orphans. An inquest will be held today.*

Accrington Times, August 19th 1876:- *On Wednesday, Vincent Loiusana, hooker-on, was killed at Messrs George Hargreaves and Co.'s Victoria coalpit. He was standing near the chain road lighting his pipe when a string of wagons laden with coal came along the tramway. A collier saw him in danger and shouted out to him, but he either did not hear or took no notice and the wagons came upon him. The first knocked him down, and his head was crushed between the second. Death was instantaneous. Loiusana was a young man from the Industrial School at Liverpool. An inquest will be held today.*

Accrington Times, January 14th 1882:- *On Monday, Mr H.J. Robinson, coroner, held an inquest at the Woodnook Inn on James Butterworth, drawer, 14, who was killed by a fall at George Hargreaves and Co's Friar Hill Pit on Thursday week. John Butterworth, labourer, of 15 Major Street, said the deceased was his son. On Thursday afternoon he had been brought home from the pit in an insensible condition, badly injured, and he died the same night. The injuries were mostly on the back of the head and on the forehead. Butterworth was dissatisfied about his son being injured, because he was sent as a drawer, and he had been employed as a labourer in removing a portion of the roof, which was not fit work for a lad of 14 to be put to. Robert Geldart, underlooker, said that about 13.30 on Thursday, he, along with Butterworth and a lad named Hindle, went into the pit to repair a chain which had thrown a number of empty wagons off the strip. While he was repairing the rails, Butterworth said there was a bit of dirt falling. Butterworth then went towards where the fall had taken place and said that there was a bit of the roof side going to fall. Geldart told him to come away, but, before Butterworth could do so, he was caught behind the shoulders by a stone about 4 foot 6 inches by 4 foot, and about 8 or 9 inches thick, and four or five pecks of stuff fell on him. He was extricated in about 10 minutes, and got out of the pit as soon as possible. He had gone of his own accord to help him put the wagons on the line. The wagons had not shaken the wall. It was 9 or 10 years since the chain road was blown. If the wagons came off the road, they generally took boys to help, but never by themselves, and boys of Butterworth's age were never sent to clear falls. Thomas Hindle, drawer, said the chain broke down and, as Butterworth had nothing to do, he went down the chain road. Geldart repaired the rails, and Hindle put 4 wagons on the line. Butterworth went below Geldart to see if the rails were right and said that a bit of the roof had fallen. He said*

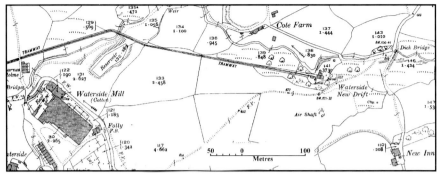

Fig.28 Waterside New Drift.

he would go and have a look, but Geldart said nothing in reply, as he was mending the rails. Hindle heard nothing else, until he found that there had been a slip. He told the coroner and jury that in no place did the wagon or chain touch the roof. Nothing was done to the part which fell. He had often gone when the chain was broken with one or more lads and a man to assist. After evidence had been given on the laying out of the body, the coroner summed up.

WATERSIDE   SD710228

Adam Bullough, a co-lessor with James Bullough of the Waterside Mill, sank this pit in 1862. By 1879 he had also developed a brick and tile works near the pithead and, according to the *List of Mines,* worked it as the Waterside Fireclay Co. In 1881, John Taylor took over the fireclay works. Coal extraction had ceased by 1886, after a brief period of working by James Hacking.[13] Thomas Knowles, of Spring Vale Fireclay Works (Taylor's Green Colliery), used the fireclay works for a period before closure in 1889. A reservoir can be seen on the site of the pit and there is a considerable heap of colliery waste on the hillside above.

Blackburn Standard, September 10th 1862:- *For some time past, Mr A. Bullough has been engaged in sinking a shaft on his estate at Waterside. On Thursday they were successful, and on Saturday he commemorated the event by giving a dinner at the Anchor Inn, Darwen Street, to about 40 of the colliers and others who have been engaged at the work.*

Blackburn Times, December 29th 1883:- *Thomas Lighbrown, collier, of Eccleshill, had his left leg broken at Mr James Hacking's Waterside Colliery yesterday morning. It was caught between the cart and the shafts. He was taken home and attended to by Dr Armitage.*

WATERSIDE NEW DRIFT   SD718236

When William Henry Shaw's Belthorn Pit was exhausted around 1900, the firm opened a drift mine near Dick Bridge, below Pickup Bank reservoir. It worked 12 inches of the Lower Mountain Mine along with a bed of fireclay, and was abandoned in 1947. A tramroad connected it with W.H. Shaw's works at Waterside. Opposite these works, a lane goes down to Victoria Building and Mill Cottages. Over the footbridge, a path on the left via a stile goes up the hill and through 2 fields before dropping down to Tinkler's Brook. At the time of writing there seemed to be an attempt to re-open the mine. Remains include 2 blocked drift entrances. The main travelling road and haulage road on the left has collapsed. The smaller (upper) drift entrance is sealed by breeze blocks, though an entrance has been made through these **(BUT DO NOT ENTER)**. The small, brick-arched opening to the side was a powder store. In front of the main drift are the remains of an engine house and haulage engine beds.

WHINNEY HILL COLLIERY   SD755303

This colliery was worked by the Altham Colliery Co., which had close connections with George, later Sir George, Macalpine. In 1878, following his marriage to the daughter of Mr Barlow, then owner of Altham Collieries, George left London and joined his father-in-law as managing partner in the firm. Then, some years before Mr Barlow's death, George Macalpine took over the management of all the Altham Collieries. As well as Whinney Hill and Moorfield Pits (in BM 58), he had charge of the Great Harwood Colliery Company and its pit at Martholme. Later, the firm acquired the Accrington Brick and Tile Works, and for many years also had the Whinney Hill Plastic Brick Co. The total number of men and boys employed at the three collieries and the brick works was 1,800. Whinney Hill Colliery, Clayton-le-Moors, dating from 1871 and working the Lower Mountain Mine, was abandoned in 1948. The *Colliery Guardian* described it as follows in 1895.

The winding engine has 2 horizontal cylinders, 20 inch in diameter by a 3 foot 6 inch stroke, made by Messrs C. Whittaker and Co. of Accrington. The drum is cylindrical, 10 foot in diameter, and 4 foot wide. The engine rises from the downcast shaft, 4 tubs in each cage of 2 decks, each tub carrying four and a half cwt. of coal. The winding ropes are one and a quarter inch in diameter, of charcoal iron. Safety catches are fitted to each cage, which are made at the colliery shops. The conductors are of pitch pine, 2 to each cage, 6 inch by 5 inch. The haulage on the main roads underground is all performed by endless chain moved by steam power. The steam engine is placed near the shaft bottom, and the boiler is nearby. The engine has 2 horizontal cylinders, 9 inch in diameter, two and a half foot stroke, geared 1 to 4. One vertical chain wheel shaft, driven by bevel gearing from the second motion shaft of the engine, actuates an endless chain working over 800 yards of haulage road to the north of the shaft. Another road, 770 yards in length to the north east of the shaft, is worked in a similar manner. The chain is carried on the tubs, which are run singular under it at definitive intervals. For ventilation, a fan of the Waddle type, 30 foot in diameter, is erected at the upcast by which Whinneyhill and Moorfield are ventilated. The fan is driven by an engine with one 18 inch horizontal cylinder, 3 foot stroke, making 72 revolutions per minute and exhausting 80,000 cubic feet of air per minute, with a 2 inch water gauge. Three Cornish boilers are in use, two 28 feet by six and a half feet, and one 28 feet by 6 feet, working pressure 50 lb. The boilers are fed by injectors, an exhaust ejector utilising the exhaust from the fan engine, a live steam ejector being kept in reserve. The boilers are hand-fired, and are covered in sand and four and a half inch brickwork. As the coal is brought to the bank, it is tipped upon a travelling conveyer made of steel plates 20 feet long by 3 foot wide. This passes it to a revolving screen of perforated steel plates 9 foot in length 4 foot diameter, with an inclination of 1 foot, which separates into cobs and rough small. The cobs fall onto a steel picking band, 15 foot by 3 foot, on which they are cleaned and delivered to a storage hopper for loading into carts. The rough small is taken by elevator to another revolving screen, same size as that named above, to separate the nuts and slack. The slack is then taken to Moorfield colliery to be coked.

A fatal accident during sinking of the colliery nearly turned into a local disaster.

Accrington Times, December 17th 1870:- An accident occurred on Saturday at the Altham Colliery Co's Whinny Hill Pit, Dyke-nook, in which 1 man was drowned and 5 men narrowly escaped. Sinking operations began here about 14 months ago and so it may be considered a new pit. There are 2 shafts, the upcast and downcast, the former being used at present to wind water, of which there is enough to need an engine running day and night to keep the other pit clear. The other shaft is being lined with bricks as required by the Act of Parliament. This work has reached the height of nearly 11 yards from the bottom, and the men engaged work off a circular scaffold, fixed to the sides and about 60 yards from the top of the pit. On Saturday, the men employed thus were James Thompson of Cockbridge, Richard Todd of Altham, John Halstead of Dyke-nook, Thomas Macintosh, underlooker, of Altham, John Wade of Clayton-le-Moors, and James Holding of the Spinner's Arms, Accrington. The bricks and mortar were let down to them by the ordinary coal tubs, and the mouth of the pit was protected by a wooden cover or jetty which works in a groove, and slides on or off as required. The jetty is barred at the sides to prevent it slipping and, when a tub has to be let down, it is raised to allow the jetty to be slid back, and then it is lowered by the engine. About noon the men at the top were pushing a tub containing 50 bricks onto the jetty to lower it into the shaft, when the bolt was seen to slip back. The jetty, the tub and its contents dashed down the pit, smashing to pieces the scaffolding, and pitching some of the men into the water below. Atkinson, the banksman, tried to hold it back, but was unable to do so. A warning was shouted from the top as the tub was seen to descend, and Thompson and Todd managed to get on to some brickwork with their knees. The other men were not so successful and were thrown into the water. Macintosh, Wade and Holding resurfaced, but Halstead was not seen to rise. Macintosh grabbed the bell wire which runs down the side of the pit, and Holding and Wade grabbed a rope lowered by the engineman. The capstan rope was lowered, and the men took hold of that. The engine rope was then hoisted up and, a tub having been attached to it, was lowered again and the men were brought up. Thompson and Todd were first, followed by Macintosh and Holding, and then Wade. Holding was hurt on the arm and had a scalp wound. The other men were injured more or less, but none fatally. Halstead's body was recovered about 16.00, and taken to Mr Bracewell's public house near by. Mr H.U. Hargreaves, coroner, held an inquest at Mr Bracewell's on Wednesday. Mr S. Dugdale was the foreman of the jury. Mr Dickinson, Inspector of Mines, was present, as was Dr Pilkington JP. Catherine Hartley, Halstead's mother, said he was born before her marriage and lived with her at Dyke-nook. He was 33 and unmarried and had worked as a collier at Whinny Hill pit only a month when the accident happened. John Atkinson, banksman, of Clayton-le-Moors, said he had just swung an empty wagon off the jetty and some other parties immediately pushed a tub containing 50 bricks onto it. By some means, the jetty moved backwards, leaving the mouth of the shaft open. The tub fell down the shaft where Halstead and 5 other men were working. The scaffolding was broken, and Halstead and 3 others were thrown into the water which was about 9 or 10 feet below and about 9 or 10 yards deep. The 5 survivors were then rescued as described above and Halstead's body was recovered some hours later. Atkinson added that the jetty should be bolted, and was bolted on this occasion, but it had been thawing and freezing, and was very slippery about the bolt, which works easy. He could not account for the jetty moving, as he was on the other side at the time. There was about a half inch of play, however, and, when the loaded tub came against the jetty, it might have jerked the bar back. The bar was back when he looked. Mr Dickinson asked if it was possible to kick the bolt out with the foot, but Atkinson said the bolt was in when he left that part of the jetty. Thomas Westwell, sinker, said he was on the brow at the time of the accident. He saw the bolt go back when the tub of bricks went on to the jetty. He was certain it was bolted before and he had never known it go back before. He told Mr Dickinson that he would not say the bolt was full up, but he could see it, as the snow did not cover the bar. John James Rippon of Altham, managing director of Altham Collieries, said the delay in recovering Halstead's body was caused by the amount of debris which fell into the pit with him. It took an hour to reduce the depth of water from 8 yards to 5 feet and he directed 2 men to search for the body. He said the platform was a very substantial one and they had calculated that the weight of the tub falling 60 yards would be equal to 47 tons, 4 cwt. He also said Atkinson was a very careful man and he thought the tub might have been partly on the jetty, but could not have been entirely, for, if it had, it would not have gone down. He did not think the bolt slipped back, neither did he think it possible for it to do so, but, according to the evidence, it would appear that it had done. Mr Dickinson asked if Mr Rippon would be justified in still using the front part of the jetty for loading if no other explanation for the accident could be given. Mr Rippon replied that, if the jetty was properly barred, there could be no danger in using the front, but he did not think it was properly barred.

141

The Coroner told him that Atkinson thought the pressure in sending on an empty tub would have driven it back, but Mr Rippon disagreed, saying that the men kept the bar well oiled for their own convenience, but he thought it could not have been in its proper place or the jetty would not have moved. The Coroner asked if the bar could be improved and Mr Rippon said he did not know. Mr Dickinson said that, if an engineer had examined these bolts, he would have considered them safe. He therefore recommended bringing the bricks and the tramway to the side. Mr Rippon replied that he would be happy to do this. Dr Pilkington told the Coroner there were no marks on Halstead's body and he had drowned. James Cronshaw, of Waterloo Street, Enfield, who laid out the body, agreed. The jury returned a verdict that Halstead was Accidentally Drowned.

Accrington Times, September 9th 1871:- The new pit at Whinney Hill is in full work. Coal and slack may be obtained at reasonable prices from Jno. Foulds, 1 Abbey Street, next to J.E. Edwards, Printers.

Accrington Times, April 26th 1873:- On Tuesday Mr Hargreaves, coroner, held an inquest at the Dog and Partridge, Hyndburn Bridge, on William Mattison, 13, drawer for Charles Redfern at Whinney Hill Coal Pit. Last Saturday morning, he was taking a wagon of coal to the ginney. He was in front of the wagon, drawing it after him, and was about 30 yards from where the coal-getter was at work when he came to an acute angle. It seems he was going too fast, for the tub jerked round and jumped him against the side, injuring him on the chest and internally. His getter went to his aid and released him, and the boy was conveyed to the pit bank and then taken home. Dr Pilkington attended, but he died from his injuries early on Sunday. The jury returned a verdict of Accidental Death.

Accrington Times, July 3rd 1880:- Thomas Rimmington, 42, collier, of South Shore Street, was killed by a roof fall at Whinney Hill pit yesterday.

Blackburn Standard, February 23rd 1889:- A fatal accident occurred at Whinney Hill Colliery, Clayton-le-Moors, when William Henry Taylor, 12, son of Robert Taylor, collier, of 8 Back House Lane, Oswaldtwistle, was working with his father in the pit. About 9.30, the lad left his father to take a wagon to the shaft bottom and, on his way there, he collided with an empty wagon in the charge of William Osborne, another drawer. The collision caused Taylor's wagon to rebound and knock him down. He was seriously injured and immediately taken home. Doctors Illingworth and Loynd attended, but their efforts were futile and he died from his injuries the next day. On Thursday an inquest was held at the Printer's Arms, Oswaldtwistle, and a verdict of Accidental Death was returned.

Accrington Advertiser, February 16th 1895:- Mr H.J. Hargreaves, coroner, held an inquest at Accrington Court Rooms on Monday on James Cooper, 57, of 38 Grange Street, who died on Thursday. His widow, Margaret

Cooper, said he worked at Whinney Hill coal-pit as a collier, until Tuesday afternoon. He complained the same evening of pain all over his body and showed her his elbow, which was all black though the skin was not broken. He told her he had fallen off his sledge. On Thursday morning she called Dr Geddie because he was much worse, but he died before the doctor arrived. Hiram Varley, sledge looker at Whinney Hill, said his job was to look after the sledges. About a fortnight ago Cooper was rather late in going out of the pit, and, on being asked why, he replied that his sledge had left the metals and thrown him off. Varley advised Cooper to have his sledge repaired, but he did not do so, and continued to use it. Dr Geddie said Cooper had died from blood poisoning. The jury's verdict reflected this, with the rider that the proprietors insist that the men have their sledges in repair.

Accrington Observer, December 7th 1895:- *On Sunday October 17th, Anthony Alex. Tomlinson, 28 and married, of 47 Henry Street, Clayton-le-Moors, met with an accident whilst working at Whinney Hill Colliery. He was cutting a road underground, when a stone measuring 6 feet by 4 slipped, and Tomlinson, who was in a stooping position, received the full weight of it on his back. The stone was removed, and Tomlinson was released by his comrades and removed to his home, and later to Blackburn Infirmary, where he died of his injuries on Thursday. An inquest was opened on Friday and, after the medical surgeon's evidence that Tomlinson had died from a rupture, the inquest was adjourned to Thursday so that the Inspector of Mines might attend. At the adjourned inquest at Blackburn, the jury returned a verdict of Accidental Death. It was stated that the stone weighed 4 cwt and needed 4 men to lift it off. A witness stated that he tried the roof on the Saturday before the accident, and it seemed quite safe.*

Accrington Observer, September 10th 1918:- *Mr D.N. Haslewood, Coroner, held an inquest at Accrington Town Hall yesterday on Leon Gambetta Booth, 40, miner, 31 Canal Street, Church, who died last Thursday from injuries received through colliding with a wood coupling, or bar, supporting the pit roof whilst returning from his work at Whinney Hill Colliery the previous Tuesday. Mr Harrison, Inspector of Mines, and Mr J. McGurk of the Miners' Federation, were present at the enquiry, and Mr Bowland appeared on behalf of the Colliery Co. William Lighbrown, miner, of 41 Henry Street, Clayton-le-Moors, said that, after finishing his work at 14.20 on Tuesday, he went on his sledge for a mile to the bottom of the rope road, where he was joined by Booth and John Thomas Tattersall, another miner. The three got in a coal tub, and had travelled some 400 or 500 yards in the direction of the pit shaft, when Booth's head hit a coupling in the roof of the main haulage road. At the time Booth was in a kneeling position in the front part of the tub, and he was thrown over the witness. The tub left the lines, and instructions were at once given for the rope which draws the tubs to be stopped. Afterwards, Booth was taken to the pit top. In reply to Mr Harrison, Lighbrown said the tubs were travelling at walking pace, around 3 miles per hour. As a rule the men sat in the tubs, two on one side and one on the other. But just when the accident occurred Booth was in a kneeling position and so his head would be a shade higher than usual. After travelling in the tub for a mile or so, the men were apt to feel the cramp, and changed their position, so that might have been the reason for Booth kneeling. Some yards before reaching this particular place, the pit was somewhat higher, and Booth might have taken advantage of that to change his position, and not have noticed when they reached the lower part. Lighbrown did not examine the bar, but it was fixed straight across and was not broken. He told Mr Roland that over 200 men had passed that place previously in safety, and if Booth had been sitting in the tub he would not have been caught. Mr McGurk pointed out that sitting on one of these tubs was not like riding on a tram car, and as a rule the men took advantage of being in a higher part of the pit to change their position for more comfort. Plans were produced, and it was shown that the height of the bar in the centre from the front of the road was about 3 feet 1 inch. It was about 2 inches lower in the centre than at the ends, the pressure having caused it to bend slightly. Mr Harrison said it would be better if the height of the bars was not less than 3 foot 6 inches. Mr McGurk suggested 4 foot 6 inches and Mr Harrison said that would be safer still. Richard Aldred, of 6 Duke Street, fireman at the pit, said he had examined the haulage road shortly before the accident, and reported all was safe. He travelled under the bars all right, and did not notice that this particular one was a little lower in the centre. If he had thought it was getting down, someone would have been put on it to warn the men until it was cut out. The men could ride easily and safely under bars 3 foot high, if they were seated in the tubs. He told Mr Rowland that Booth had a lamp, and could have seen the bar if he had paid attention. 258 men had gone under safely just before the accident. Herbert Mercer, another workman, stated that after the accident Booth was taken to the pit top and attended to by Dr Watson. He was afterwards taken to Victoria Hospital. Mercer had been working on this road for 12 months, and the bar had been there all the time. He had not noticed any difference in the bar and, if Booth had been sitting, he would not have been struck at all. Nurse Grove, of Victoria Hospital, said Booth had suffered a fracture of the spine and died from his injuries at 1.00 a.m. on Thursday. Mr Harrison pointed out that Booth might have misjudged the height of the bar and added that it was not unusual for the men to brush their heads against the bars without any serious consequences. The Coroner said he agreed with Inspector's suggestion that it would be better if the bars could be raised a little bit. Mr Harrison stated that when the bar was cut away after the accident, it straightened out, and this showed that the bend was due to pressure. Mr Rowland said there had never been such an accident at the pit previously. Booth was one of the best workmen the company had ever had, and had been a fine example to other employees. The Coroner opined that the occurrence was a pure accident. Some discussion took place as to the advantage of warnings being issued to the men with regard to the danger, but Mr Harrison did not think this was necessary. The accident itself would serve as a warning. A verdict of Accidental Death was returned.*

The *List of Mines* for 1896 shows William and C. Shaw and Co. working this pit, with Charles E. Arthur as colliery manager and Robert Vickery as under-manager. Only 3 men worked underground, with 2 on the surface, probably on maintenance, for the colliery was abandoned on June 12th 1895. Nearly 25,000 gallons of water per day was pumped out of the workings after the pit was abandoned. The site of this colliery, to the right of the Red Lion public house at Whitebirk, is now occupied by an oil distributor.

Blackburn Standard, December 30th 1882:- *Re the Darwen Mining Company Limited by order of the Liquidators. To be sold by auction at the Old Bull Hotel, Blackburn at 6 p.m. on Monday, January 8th 1883, by Messrs Salisbury and Hamer as a going concern, the Whitebirk Colliery, near Blackburn, together with fixed and loose machinery, plant and effects in and about the same, including 2 double winding machines, 2 pumping engines, 3 boilers, about 200 tram wagons, horse and cart, office furniture, 40 coke ovens, boilers for cisterns, crabs, and other requisites for working. The collieries are held under 3 leases, dated 1872, 1874, and 1875, which can be inspected at the office of the solicitors to the Liquidators. The minimum rents and royalties are moderate in amount. There are about 4,000 tons of coal upon which royalty is payable. The shaft and all the working plant and fixtures, which have cost altogether about £18,000 and are of the most substantial character, are upon the Estates of Jonathan Peel, Esq, and the coal included in the lease from him can be worked out in about 5 years, whilst the coal in one of the other leases can be worked out in about 2 years. The purchaser will have the option of taking a transfer of all or any of the leases. A valuable stream of water issues from the mine and, until a few months ago, was sold to Blackburn Corporation at a rental of £1,300 per annum. At the pit shaft this water is at such an elevation as will enable it to be taken by force gravitation either to Blackburn, Church or Oswaldtwistle, and, as the water is of a superior quality for drinking or manufacturing purposes, a considerable revenue may be obtained from it. The colliery is almost the only one working within easy reach of these populous towns, where most of the coal is sold. Further particulars may be had on application to the Liquidators, Mr C.J. Beckett, Clarence Cottage, Over Darwen, and Mr Doctor Pickup, Higher Lawrence Street, Over Darwen; from the Auctioneers, Church Street Blackburn, or from F.G. Hindle, solicitor, Darwen, Lancashire.*

Blackburn Standard, April 14th 1883:- *The Over Darwen Industrial Co-operative Society Limited are in want of a thoroughly competent person (certified) to take on the management of their Whitebirk Colliery, near Blackburn. The seam now being worked is the Half Yard or Mountain Mine, and none but those who have had some practical experience in working this series need apply. The person appointed will be likewise required to reside in close proximity to the colliery. Apply in person at the Board Rooms,*

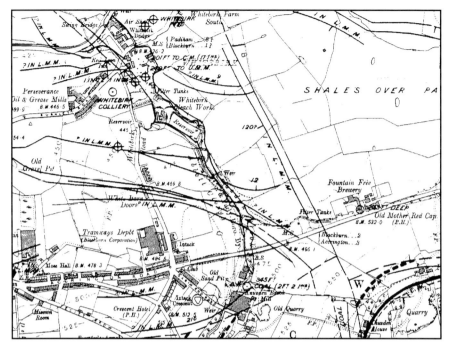

Fig.29 Whitebirk Colliery.

*Central Stores, School Street, Over Darwen on Wednesday evening next,
April 18th at 7 o'clock. C.J. Beckett, Secretary.*

Accrington Times, January 17th 1885:- *On Saturday an explosion of firedamp
occurred at Whitebirk Colliery, Blackburn, injuring 3 young men. There
were between 80 and 90 men in the mine, and it is said that one of them
opened his lamp in order to re-light the lamp of a drawer. Immediately an
explosion of firedamp occurred. Both men were burnt about the head, and
another drawer was knocked down by the force of the explosion, and injured
about the head and arms. The manager, Mr William Taylor, was at the
shaft top when he heard the explosion, and he at once went down and directed
all his attention to getting the men out. When their safety had been assured,
he had the fire extinguished before much damage was done to the mines.
The workings, then being filled with chokedamp, were abandoned pending an
inspection. Dr Wilson was sent for to attend the injured men, who were then
sent to their respective homes. The explosion was a comparatively slight one.*

Blackburn Standard, February 14th 1885:- *William Taylor, manager of
Whitebirk Colliery, appeared before J. Lewis and W. Astley Esq at the
Borough Police Courts on Thursday to answer a summons charging him
with neglecting to appoint an inspector of the coal mine at Whitebirk, on
the 10th ult. Mr Holden, of Bolton, prosecuted, and Mr Brothers defended.*

146

Mr Holden said he appeared on behalf of Mr Dickinson, the Chief Inspector of Mines, and the prosecution was ordered by the Home Office, in consequence of the laxity of the management in Whitebirk Colliery, which belonged to the Over Darwen Industrial Co-operative Society. An accident occurred there on January 10th and two days later, when Mr Martland, an inspector, visited the pit, he found that a competent person had not been appointed to take the management. It appeared that in early January, the fireman and another of the officials of the pit fell ill. A youth named Smith, who had assisted the regular fireman, was temporarily appointed. Safety lamps were used throughout the mine, and one of the lamp stations was at a point where the drawing road communicated with another road. On the morning of January 10th, when an explosion took place, a man called Howson was entrusted with the keys of the lamps. He travelled from the shaft along the chain road a considerable distance when he lost his light. He called along the chain road for a light and Smith, who could neither read or write, went along the drawing road and sent Silcock, a collier, to give Howson a light. Unfortunately, there was a considerable amount of gas there at the time and, when the light was given, an explosion occurred. There was no loss of life and the 2 men who were injured were recovering. There was what appeared to be a mismanagement in the pit and, from the report book and statements made at the time of the examination, it was manifest that Mr Taylor, in the absence of a proper fireman, had not taken proper precautions in appointing a person to replace the sick fireman. It was apparent that the temporary fireman, Smith, had not done his duty in inspecting the whole of the roadways and, in neglecting to do this, it plainly showed he was not a competent person as was required by the Act. Mr Martland, Inspector of Mines, said he had visited the mine 2 days after the explosion and made a report of the cause and circumstances attending it. Mr Brothers admitted the offence, but pleaded extenuating circumstances. He said Smith had worked in the pit over 6 years and had frequently accompanied the fireman on his rounds and the manager had gone down with Smith every morning before the accident. The Bench fined the defendant £5 and costs, and hoped it would be a warning to him and others.

Blackburn Standard, March 5th 1887:- William Haworth, assistant fireman, of Hermitage Street, Rishton, was summoned by William Taylor, colliery manager for Darwen Mining Co., at the Borough Police Court yesterday for having, on the 23rd ult. in Whitebirk Colliery, worked with a light other than a locked safety lamp, contrary to the Coal Mines Regulations Act, 1872. At noon on the above date, the defendant unscrewed his lamp in a part of the pit where there is dangerous gas. The consequence was that there was a slight explosion, and Haworth's face was singed. Mr Radcliffe, defending, said Haworth did not deny the offence, but pleaded that the explosion occurred in a most unlikely place, where the accumulation of gas was not expected, and that he had sustained bodily injury. He asked that the Bench be as lenient as they could. The Bench said it was a very serious case, but only fined the defendant 19s. and costs, seeing that he had been injured.

A description of the pit appeared in a Blackburn paper in 1888 in an article on coalmining at Whitebirk, with a history of the colliery which had then been working for almost 16 years.

Blackburn Weekly Express, Saturday, June 30th 1888:- *In 1865 the father of the present manager of Whitebirk Colliery conducted boring operations on the Peel estate at Whitebirk, with a view to finding coal or any other mineral which might exist. Coal was found in apparently large quantities, but at that time nothing more was done towards getting it. In 1870 or 1871 Mr William Taylor, the present manager, floated a company to work it and 2 shafts were sunk, occupying the men for 18 months working day and night. Since the shafts were completed, the colliery has been in full work and many thousands of tons have been procured from it. The company, called the Darwen Mining Co., did not flourish, however, and they put a mortgage on the colliery of £6,000. In 1883 they went into voluntary liquidation and the Darwen Industrial Co-operative Society Ltd, who had the mortgage, were left with the colliery. They determined to work it, and have done so ever since, becoming the only Co-operative Society in England ever successfully to work a coal mine. When they took over, the coal under the Peel estate was nearly worked out, and fresh workings have been carried out under land belonging to Lieut-General Fielden, GMG, MP. They work the Lower Mountain Mine and the seam is about 2 feet thick, dipping about 3 inches to the yard. The extent of the workings already in existence is about 1,300 yards, and employment is found for 140 men and boys. When our reporter visited the mine this week, Mr Taylor, the manager, took him through the workings. All the engines and boilers for hoisting and pumping are on the pit bank and the 5 engines are variously employed. Two are used for hoisting the cage containing the men and the coal at the upcast shaft, and one for pumping the water out of the lower workings, where it congregates in large quantities, by means of the downcast shaft. Another is kept in reserve and, for the sake of economy in fuel, a small one is used to drive the larger one pumping the water. The large engine pumps about 500 or 600 gallons of water per minute out of the mine, and this is sold to the Leeds and Liverpool Canal Company. The cage is in the form of a large box without sides or ends. The bottom of it is wood, and iron bars form supports at each side, while the ends are left open. On the way down, the cage rushes through the air at a terrific rate, then there seems to be a sudden stop and a reversal of the process and the cage seems to start to ascend the pit shaft. All is in darkness, for the Davy lamps give but little light at first, but at last we found ourselves safely at the shaft bottom, having accomplished 137 yards in 19 seconds. This however is not reckoned to be a very quick rate of progress, as the cage, when it contains coal, goes up in 12 or 13 seconds. Nothing could be seen for a few minutes, until the eye got used to the changed conditions, and then a couple of men could be dimly observed engaged in running the trucks of coal into the cage ready to be hoisted to the pit mouth. There is a gradual slope from the workings to the shaft bottom, and the trucks of coal can be brought along a chain road running parallel with the intake airway without any labour or steam whatever. An endless chain runs from the workings to the pit mouth. Each truck is fitted with a fork in which the chain catches and runs the coal truck from one end of the mine to the other. As the ground dips towards the shaft, the weight of the trucks causes them to work without any additional power being applied. The air supply is very good, being regulated by means of a large open furnace, situated at what is now the back of the upcast shaft. By increasing or decreasing the fire in the furnace, a stronger or weaker current of air can be procured. The air comes down the mine via the downcast shaft, up which the water is pumped and which is seldom used, and it travels through the workings, finally escaping up the upcast shaft, in which the cage is constantly working and at the bottom of which is the furnace. The miners travel on small flat sledges, travelling along the intake airway, running parallel with the chain road*

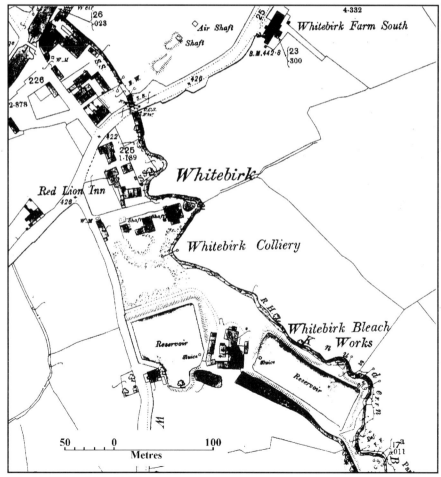

Fig.30 Whitebirk Colliery.

149

PLATE XXI The only known photograph of Whitebirk Colliery, seen behind the launching of a barge (Blackburn Reference Library).

and, in some parts, the waterway. In very few places it is more than 4 feet high and 2 yards wide. After about 650 yards, there is a rather sudden drop of about 9 feet, caused through a fault in the seam. The miners, however, knew the signs and had blasted the rock to find the seam started again 9 feet below. This fault was discovered about 5 years ago, and 2 years later another fault was found about 250 yards higher up the intake. This fault had, however, taken an upward tendency and the seam was found about 5 feet higher. We followed the intake airway for a very long time, but finally a deviation was made along one of the many passages running out of it. All these borings lead to different parts of the workings and, where they leave the main road, they are fitted with doors and brattice cloths so that too strong a current of air may not get into them at once. After travelling nearly 1,300 yards, a portion of the workings was reached at which was fixed another roller carrying the endless chain, where the men hook on the trucks which are then received by the hooker at the shaft bottom and placed into the cage ready to be hoisted to the mouth of the pit. These trucks are run directly from the miners by boys who work with little or no clothing on them, and who seem to revel in running about on the rough floor with bare feet. These youngsters, whose ages vary from 12 to 16, are in very few cases Blackburn boys. The people in this district prefer to send their lads to the mill, where they can go a couple of years earlier and where they can earn more money from the start, rather than to the mine. Boys have to be got, *however, and most of those working at Whitebirk come from the schools of Liverpool. Very few of them would leave mining once they got used to the work and the surroundings. After drawing for 3 or 4 years these lads are put on getting coal and a short time after become fully fledged miners.*

After watching the drawers, we went along one of the cuttings to where the men were getting the coal. This is done by fully fledged miners only. They are the men who make the cuttings running off the main road and, to do this, they have to subject themselves to great discomfort. Like the boys they discard any clothing, which would only get in their way, and in a position, which can only described as two double, pursue their arduous and risky duties. Every 6 yards they start a cutting of 4 yards wide and about 2 feet 10 inches high. These cuttings are proceeded with for about 40 yards, then a fresh cutting is made 6 yards higher up the main road. In making these cuttings, the miners use nothing but the pick and a large sledge hammer. First of all they pick away at the shale which lies beneath the seam and, when they have removed enough, they bring the sledge hammer and chisel into play to remove the large cobs of coal from the seam. As they proceed along the cutting the miners insert pillars of wood to support the roof. When they have worked to the end of the seam, or to the boundary of their land, they start to work back. This is done by cutting away at the pillars of 6 yards wide which were left as supports when they first worked along the colliery. The earnings of a collier are only very modest when one considers the amount of work they have to do and the dangers they have to run. A good collier working full time will be able to earn about 30s. per week, but the average is between 20s. and 25s. Their hours are limited to 9 a day, but it is only in very few cases that the men put in the full time. They go down the mine at 6.00 a.m. and are kept there until noon, when they can leave for the day or continue to work. Before the passing of the Coal Mines Act last year, the miners were paid so much per truck for the coal they got, but under the new Act they get paid by weight. The coal is weighed at the pit-mouth by the banksman and is sorted into classes, by riddling or screening. What coal is left after the first screening is known as best-cottage coal, the second screening as second cottage, and the third as slack or nuts for mills and manufacturers. For blacksmiths and forges the coal is specially sorted and consequently dearer. The lamps at Whitebirk are encased Davy's. With the miners at this pit the Davy lamp has always been viewed with great favour, but the management, anxious to have the best, tried the Morgan and Marsaut safety lamps. The men however did not take kindly to them, and the Davy was put into general use.

Blackburn Standard, September 30th 1893:- The miners at Whitebirk Colliery, near Blackburn, numbering about 50, have resumed work at the old rates of wages, and they are now working 3 shifts per day in order to cope with orders. These colliers have been members of the Federation about 10 years, during which time they contributed 3d. per week to the union funds, but in return have only received 5s. for one week during the strike. The men are now seriously thinking of forming a union of their own.

151

PLATE XXII The ginney track on Hoddlesden Moss, ca.1950.

WINTER HILL   SD670233

There are no fewer than a dozen coal workings near the summit of Winter Hill, in Over Darwen, dating from at least the 1840s. Slight hollows in the area indicate remains of mining and, to the south of Stepback Farm there is a capped mine shaft. Coal Pit House Farm also suggests former mining activities. The following extract from the *Report on Child Labour in Coal-Mines 1841* gives the ownership of the mine in the 1840s:-

Mr Mark Townley, Winter Hill Coal-mine, District of Over Darwen, township of Tockholes, parish of Blackburn. Children: 1 of 11 years, 1 of 12 years. None can write, both can read and attend Sunday school and public worship. Wages average 5 shillings. Young persons: 1 of 13 and 1 of 14. One can write, both can read and both attend Sunday school and public worship. Wages average 6 shillings per week. Number of adults: 8. All the above are drawers, they draw by the belt and chain. The length of the run is about 60 yards. The weight of coal 1 cwt. The height of the headings is 2 feet. There is no firedamp in this mine, and no loss of life or injury has been sustained by any accident for the past 2 years.

WOOD NOOK   SD760279

A Hargreaves, Ashworth and Co's colliery where drift mining began in the Lower Mountain Mine circa 1830, using pit ponies for haulage, Wood Nook was later worked by George Hargreaves and Co. Air shafts for ventilating the pit and for secondary access were located on Rothwell Heights and Shoe Mills. The Lower Mountain Mine was abandoned in 1897, but reopened in 1923 for 4 years whilst pillars supporting the chain haulage road running to Millers Fold Pit were removed.[2] The colliery employed 20 miners underground and 3 men on the surface in 1896, when Nathan Haworth was manager.

Bacup and Rossendale Times, February 24th 1866:- *Colliers employed by Messrs Hargreaves, Ashworth and Co. (Wood Nook and Baxenden Collieries) have received an advance of 6d. per quarter, equal to 10.5% on the previous rates paid to them, while colliers employed by the Trustees of the late Joseph Barnes, Church, and Messrs Simpson and Co., Oswaldtwistle, have received a 10% advance. The price of coals at the various pits have risen in proportion!*

Accrington Times, March 1st 1873:- *Sir, The coal question is the cry of the day, England over, and also how to economise this precious fuel. You will undoubtedly hear loud complaints about the dissolute habits of colliers, and that they won't attend their work more than 2 or 3 days per week, because they are in receipt of good wages. Some people say this is the principal cause why coal is so scarce. They do not take into consideration the fact that of late years the demand has greatly increased, while the supply has not kept pace with it. What is the cause of this? The great increase in our population, and the coal required for home consumption in the manufacture of iron etc. have had a great affect on the market. Yet I believe that the chief cause is that the colliers have been miserably paid in the past. Parents could see it would be to their advantage to send their boys to other work than the coal-pit, work which would be more profitable, for in addition to poor wages, they have been incarcerated in the pit like a prison house for 12 or 13 hours at once, and in the winter season only see daylight once a week. Explosions and falls of roof take away annually 1,000 lives, and their ranks have not been filled up with young recruits, consequently the great army of labour in this particular branch has dwindled down. The inevitable result of this has been that the supply has equalled the demand. When coal was being supplied to large consumers at from 4s 6d to 5 shillings per ton, the coal owners' profits were small. Colliers' wages then were very low, so that the public were getting supplied with cheap coal, whilst the producers were struggling with poverty. Coals are now a fearful price, and the wonder is, when will they stop? For, although coal is scarce, is there any necessity for advancing the price of this precious commodity any higher than it is? Coals have risen in the last few days from 2 shillings to 3 shillings per ton, and they have offered the colliers 10% of an advance, or what is equivalent to 1 shilling for 2 tons 8 cwt of coal. So the public will*

PLATE XXIII Shaft sinkers at top of Hoddlesden No.12 shaft, ca.1932.

be able to judge who is getting the lion's share, for while the coal owners are raising the price of coal 2 shillings a quarter they offer their men 1 shilling. The men resent such an offer as this and are determined to have 15%, which is equal to 1s 6d.

Accrington Times, March 8th 1873:- *The carters in Accrington have long been dissatisfied with the remuneration they have received for carting coals, for, whilst almost everything has been advancing for the last 2 years, they have continued to cart at about the same rate as they did when times were good and horses, carts and provender were cheap compared with their prices now. A horse that could have been got for £30 two years ago costs now about £50, and carts that could have been purchased for £15 cannot be had for much less than £20, and so with other requisites in more or less proportion. Again the length of time carters have to wait for coals has caused them, or their employers, a great amount of loss and trouble. Occasionally carters have gone to the pits by one in the morning, while it has been a common thing to go at four or five in order to be served first with coals. And although they have gone so early, they have not been able to obtain as many coals by 3 or 4 loads a day as they would have done if coals had been good to get. Several carters, therefore, have raised their prices of carting cottage coals from Whinney Hill and Wood Nook from 1 penny to 3 half pence per cwt. and some of the manufacturers sympathising with their carters of steam coals have given them 4 pence per ton in advance.*

Accrington Times, July 7th 1877:- *Minutes of Accrington Local Board of Health Wood Nook Tip. Mr B. Hargreaves said he had got a draft of a meeting and agreement from Messrs George Hargreaves, and they stipulated that the board remove the soil and, when filled, cover over with ashes. They also stipulated for the privilege of tipping matter from the coal mines or any other place. They might bring stuff 2 miles, and he thought that they should confine themselves to engine refuse.*

YATEBANK   SD713232

Blackburn Newspaper, March 1844:- *Henry Sharples, 9, was found dead with his head cut open at the bottom of John Clayton's mine at Yate Bank, Darwen. Clayton was prosecuted under the new Act, and fined £5, despite the fact that Sharples had been employed in another mine since the age of 7, and was thus employed in a mine before the Act came in.*

SOURCES

1. Crossley, R.S. "Accrington Captains of Industry" (Accrington: Wardleworth, 1930).

2. Dickinson, J. & Martin, J.S. "*The Collieries of Lancashire in 1879*"

3. Rothwell, M. *Industrial Heritage, A guide to the Industrial Archaeology of Church and Oswaldtwistle, including the villages of Belthorn, Knuzden, and Stanhill* (1993).

4 Dickinson, J. *Statistics of The Collieries of Lancashire, Cheshire and North Wales* (1854)

5. Inventory of Peter Wright Pickup. I am grateful to Gordon Hartley of Burnley, for permission to use extracts from this inventory.

6. Abram, William A. *History of Blackburn Town and Parish* (1877), page 492

7. Abbott, V. *Pictorial History of Hoddlesden.*

8. *Blackburn Times*, April 27th 1929, page 13, col. 3. "Alsatian dog that was left for dead"

9. Rothwell, M. *Industrial Heritage, A Guide to the Archaeology of Darwen, including Hoddlesden, Yate and Pickup Bank, Eccleshill and Tockholes* (Darwen: 1992).

10. Ned Clarke *Once Upon A Mine* (Burnley: Clarke: 1997).

11. Gordon Hartley *Coal Mining in Blackburn*, typescript, Blackburn Reference Library.

12. Geological Survey, Accrington reference library.

13. Catalogue of Plans of Abandoned Mines

Accrington Library: Trade Directories, Accrington Newspapers, 1858 onwards. Local Photograph collection, OS Maps, and newspaper cuttings.

Blackburn Library: Newspapers 1793 onwards.

Burnley Library: Newspapers 1852, onwards, Trade Directories. OS Maps.

Darwen Library: Darwen Newspapers, 1876 onwards, OS Maps, and newspaper cutting collection.

Lancashire Mining Museum, Buile Hill, Eccles Old Road, Salford. Mining Records, Colliery Year Books, Mines Inspectors Reports etc.

Mining Records: *Catalogue of Plans of Abandoned Mines for North East Lancashire.*

INDEX OF PERSONAL NAMES

Cronshaw, James	142	Green, James	120
Crossley, R.S.	10	Greenhalgh, A.F. Mr	38
Cunliffe, James	69	Greenwood, Ernest	33
		Greenwood, Mary Ann	33
Davies, Alan	8	Gregson, John	120
Davies, John	86	Griffiths, Peter	116
Davies, Mr	83	Griffiths, William	116
Dean, J. Mr	134	Grime, Mr	19
Derbyshire, James	83	Grimshaw, Mr	25, 32, 105
Dickinson, Joseph	42, 83, 90	Grimshaw, Richard	96
Dickinson, Mr	15, 23, 29, 31, 32	Grumm, William Henry	33
	38, 43, 46, 61, 66		
	105	Hacking, James	138
Dobson, Henry Neville	114	Halewood, Mr	113
Dodd, Henry	113	Hall, Hubert	114
Dooley, Patrick	130	Hall, Jonathan	10
Duckworth, (Councillor)	22	Hall, Mr	69
Duckworth, J. Mr	76, 118	Halliwell, Albert	119
Duckworth, John	40, 42, 43, 84	Halstead, John	140
Duckworth, Thomas	83	Hamer, John	33
Duerden, John	120	Hamer, William Henry	33
Duxbury, John	66	Hammond, L. Mr	76
Duxbury, Thomas	14, 15	Hargreaves, George	10, 11, 21, 22, 29
		Hargreaves, H.U. Mr	31, 52, 61, 96
East, Robert	42	Hargreaves, Henry	10
Eastham, George	40	Hargreaves, J. Mr	19, 29, 39, 42
Eastwood, John	45	Hargreaves, James	97
Eccles, Joseph	20, 120	Hargreaves, John	69, 83
Eccles, William	66	Hargreaves, Mr	14, 28, 31, 38, 46
Edleston, Thomas	18	Harrison, Mr	110
Egan, George	127	Harrison, Richard	32
Ellis, Radcliffe A. (Major)	113	Harrison, Thomas	117
Ellison, John	83	Hartley, Catherine	141
Entwistle, James	52	Hartley, Gordon	8, 109
Entwistle, John	29, 30, 52	Hartley, James Edward	50
Entwistle, Ralph	37	Hartley, Joseph	130
Entwistle, Robert	121	Hartley, Peter	14
Entwistle, Thomas	101	Harwood, John	9
Entwistle, William	84, 121	Harwood, Michael	38
Extwistle, Richard	52	Harwood, Richard	38
		Harwood, Thomas	101
Faramond, Joseph	110	Haslewood, D.N. Mr	38, 143
Fearan, (P.S.)	41	Haworth, Charles	129
Finch, Tom	77	Haworth, Dr	84
Fish, Benjamin	89	Haworth, George	84, 90
Fisk, J.	47	Haworth, James	29
Fleming, Jonathan	54, 92	Haworth, Joseph	84
Fletcher, Daniel	86	Haworth, Nathan	26, 33, 71, 97
Forrest, William	20	Haworth, William	147
Fort, Richard	53	Hayes, Henry	131
Foulds, Jonathan	142	Hayworth, Dennis	13
Garvey, (D.S.)	33	Hazlewood, D.N. Mr	113
Geddie, Dr	34	Henry, Sharples	155
Geldard, Robert	136, 137	Hilton, Richard	56
Gerrard, J. Mr	38	Hindle, F. Mr	50
Gerrard, Mr	20, 33, 50, 66	Hindle, F.G. Mr	61
	67	Hindle, James	19, 83, 102
Gordon, C. Mr	73	Hindle, Richard	22
Gorton, George	117	Hindle, Thomas	30, 137
Gorton, Thomas	42	Hindle, William	82